GENESIS OUT OF DARKNESS INTO THE LIGHT

Dakoda Blue

BALBOA.
PRESS

A DIVISION OF HAY HOUSE

Balboa Press books may be ordered through booksellers or by contacting:

Balboa Press
A Division of Hay House
1663 Liberty Drive
Bloomington, IN 47403
www.balboapress.com
1 (877) 407-4847

Because of the dynamic nature of the Internet, any web addresses or links contained in this book may have changed since publication and may no longer be valid. The views expressed in this work are solely those of the author and do not necessarily reflect the views of the publisher, and the publisher hereby disclaims any responsibility for them.

The author of this book does not dispense medical advice or prescribe the use of any technique as a form of treatment for physical, emotional, or medical problems without the advice of a physician, either directly or indirectly. The intent of the author is only to offer information of a general nature to help you in your quest for emotional and spiritual well-being. In the event you use any of the information in this book for yourself, which is your constitutional right, the author and the publisher assume no responsibility for your actions.

Any people depicted in stock imagery provided by Thinkstock are models, and such images are being used for illustrative purposes only. Certain stock imagery © Thinkstock.

Print information available on the last page. .

ISBN: 978-1-4525-1423-9 (sc)
ISBN: 978-1-4525-1422-2 (e)

Balboa Press rev. date: 05/12/2015

As we expose painful events written or spoken the mind is able to start a real cleansing process. Washing away the dirt and fifth via many tears (a real wash out), or download. Though others may feel angry about the information exposed this is not the focus of my writings. The words are truly meant to heal those directly affected. I am not saying that no hurt is bought to those involved; I'm merely stating that to heal requires a lot of dirty laundry to be cleaned up. Painful as it may be the end results will always bring some peace to the victim. As long as these feelings are trapped in the mind the person can never have a free spirit. So to me the message must be delivered and received with intelligence. If abuse can destroy a person's future or alter the outcome, then the importance of prevention must be shouted out. Yet abuse is constantly at risk in our world of mental immaturity. How do we deal with this vast problem is what we need to explore deeply. A troubled mind can cause or inflict so much on the innocent prey.

Because of my abuse I was left being an over sensitive person to the needs of others. My problem was that hearing a persons problems pulled me into their resolution. We cannot take the world's problems on our shoulders. Because of this I have assisted to many individuals before solving my own problems. I can see that now lack of self-love is what I call it. I pray that God will send me a cure for this world spread affliction. As I have rehashed my writings I do say that my story is short. I do not want to bore you because I don't appreciate long stories. This was a brief synapse of who I am. There are many more events that led me into this being that I am. I just wanted to share some of the reasons a person can be led into a certain direction. For Example, women who seem to care for their boyfriends or husbands more than themselves are sometimes preyed upon. I try to put my children first because God knows my thoughts may not have always portrayed this. A parent must be willing to sacrifice for their children, if this is not a part of your protocol than you should think several times and act appropriate to prevent parenthood. The responsibilities of a parent, and those tending to our children is merely one foundation of my goals in helping the adults of tomorrow; the children and young people of today.

As I write down thoughts of my earlier years, I will dive into the past, present and future. Thinking back on my yester years I can now relate and evaluate the actions of myself and others. As they say, I can see clearly now. Years ago I might have had different ideas for my actions seeing more faults now. It's usually easier and less painful to look back. In life as we search through past events we can get a chance to mend fences and create bridges to connect our lives with goals created to become successful. If even success merely mean knowing our selves.

My name is Patricia Ann Boyd, born Patricia Ann Rice. I was born August 21, 1949 in Staten Island Hospital on Staten Island, NY. I was the first born to an 18 year old African American woman named Ruth Rice. Ruth L. Rice I believe that might have E before it: Ruthel. My Aunt Bae used to call my mother "Love". As I think back I see how she longed for and needed love. Ruth was the youngest child born into the union of Reily, my grandfather and Catherine, my grandmother. To my understanding Catherine died approximately nine months after giving birth to Ruth. You see older people were taught to be tight lipped. You had to sometimes pull information out of them. They grew up knowing how to keep their lips sealed. I believe Catherine died from Tuberculosis. Back in the 1930's this was a deadly disease to the lungs; very infectious. Medical Care wasn't advanced and not easily obtained to the lower income people of the South. I was also told that my great grandfather was born into slavery. So I would assume that his land in the South was a product of the forty acres and a mule given to the freed slaves. As a young man with four children, living back than 1930's I cannot even begin to visualize the difficulties my grandfather faced as a single parent. I know that when I was only six years old I can remember my family picking cotton. So he truly needed help with child care. As a result of this my mother and her siblings were cared for by her maternal grandmother. This put my mother on a path that she rode for many years before settling down in New York City in Staten Island. I would venture out and say that this took toll on my mother's mental development. She believed that as a child she had polio, affecting one limb. That leg she used a walking stick for, until one day an old lady told her to start using that leg before it became contracted. She obeyed and the family threw away the crutch. That was a good thing because to this day my mother cannot remember which leg was affected. A mother teaches us so much. Things that only a female can contribute in her graceful ways. Grandmothers' care now for their grandchildren more because their own children are absent due to aids drug abuse etc. Back then so much technology was not available. Washing machines, in some cases, indoor bathrooms, and well water was used, etc.

A mother's gentle touch of reassurance can comfort us giving us a sense of warmth and caring. One that makes us sense that all is not lost. A mother's smile can tear down barriers that children have built up in self-defense for self preservation.

Dads, I am not down playing you. I grew up without a father. I was forever searching for a strong steady arm to hold me. I never really felt a full sense of protection that a dad can provide. That firm strong hand of authority that also generates a radiant fatherly love that many women never stop searching for. You can find a man but his qualities are most of the times governed by his real relationship with his father or lack of fatherhood. This is a phenomenon I cannot go into now (I'm a girl) Men know what they get or got from good fathers or were not treated fairly by substitute dads. Some never realize what they lacked.

Getting back on track my grandfather made a decision that others might not have made. Each person in life decides to follow a path that does not always deliver the best results for all. As a result my mother had a pressured relationship with her father. I believe she found it very hard to forgive him for starting a new family without her and her siblings. I don't know if she ever forgave him. As events unfold in life some of us are affected differently. Some children grow up and out; some become fixated a turn inward, their emotions lost in turmoil. Their growth can be effected tremendously. I believe that my mother felt lonely and abandoned. A room can be full but without a sense of well-being you can feel all alone. This type of emotional trauma can lead to deep stressors. Responses to these buried stressors can trigger later in life. At this time we cannot explain nor predict our actions, or reactions. So I might say after growing up like this, then why would she send 3 of her own children back to the South to be cared for by relatives? Having to be shipped off to her grandmother to live had an impact on my mother. We don't always relate one situation to another on a conscious level. Then I have to realize that each of us has circumstances that lead us in directions that might not be our first nor best choice. Because of either, the lack of knowledge or mere ignorance my mother had three children and was not married. This is neither a crime nor a negative statement. It's a fact back in those days she could not have cared for three children as a single parent and worked. My father was a sperm donor for many children and my mother was only one of the many women that he had. Abortions were few and costly. Most abortions were done in the back rooms without proper equipment or proper care. I thank God that I'm here. I guess it was easier to send her kids south and continue working up in the North where the opportunities were greater.

The family I was sent to live with in the south was the Browning family. My uncle, whom I called daddy like his children did, was my only father figure. He was tall, dark, handsome, strong, kind and loving. He would sometimes ride me on his shoulder and his son on the other shoulder. People thought that my cousin Boe and I were twins. We were a year apart in age. I felt a sense of belonging. In my heart, I was in their family, not a niece, or a cousin, but a daughter and a sister.

Though years later, I wondered how they really felt about me. They had one more mouth to feed. My mother would occasionally come to see me, sending me gifts from New York. I can remember a toy doll, a walking doll, you pull her arm and she walked. A butter fly inside of a ball that was attached to a stick. As you rolled the ball the butterfly's wings flapped, I think it lit up. Daddy had country like manners. He had a smile that could penetrate your sadness. He was a strong old school man. Later I sought out quite a few tall men.

We've come this far by faith. This is the story of my life. It's a theme I've had in my heart for a long time. Living with my aunt and uncle meant a lot to me as a person, as a child, as a human being. Little did I know that my equilibrium would be disrupted when at the age of 6 years old my mother would come to take me to New York. We must build up a child's confidence; give them a sense of well-being. New York swallowed me up took my core. For me: going to New York was scary.

I was leaving with a mother who only birthed me. The day I was about to leave the South, I can still remember going out into my grandmother's front yard alone. I was looking up into the trees, feeling so much alone.

Feeling so hurt, why was I being pulled from the arms of this caring family? Feeling weak with sadness as I looked up I noticed an elf sitting in the tree. To this day, I will stand by what I saw. Was it really, real? To me it was because the most calming effect came over me. A feeling that everything would be alright. Maybe this was God's way of protecting me from further mental trauma at this moment. I then did not resist the journey. It was a long car ride to New York. None of it I can remember now. Family to me has always had deep meaning. Living in New York changed my life, leading me into a path that I am now trying to detour and branch out.

Being robbed of my virginity and sense of balance at age six was traumatic for me. I told no one, I believe I buried this deep in my mind, erased it for a short time. The problem with this technique is that we forget the good events in the process. Alcohol and its availability triggered this event, you see my mother's boyfriend spent the night with us, and I say us because we had one room, one bed. I slept at the foot of the bed. When my mother got up to go to work he was still asleep so she left him there. She left me in the bed with a stranger as far as I was concerned. As a parent this was a No No. We need to foresee what can be done to our children left with a stranger. You can understand why from a young age I never wanted to mess with alcohol. Alcohol can contribute to unwanted behavior. It will lower your inhibitions. Today alcohol abuse is a major problem. With the stressors in our life today and yesterday's many people use alcohol as an antidote. They think that alcohol will make them calmer, maybe, but how many people know their limit or know how much alcohol will create unwanted responses. As people drink day in and day out, there are so many fatalities; especially around the holidays. It's the holidays when people use this as a reason to drink (who am I). You cannot drown your thoughts; they will return later. We as human beings must find appropriate ways to face our demons; not flood them with alcohol. Many people are in denial that they even have a drinking problem. They say, "Oh I can stop whenever I want to; I drink because I like to I want to". Yea ok! Fool yourself.

Know when to get professional help. Some people are more sensitive to the effect of alcohol. When alcoholism runs in families, be cautious when drinking. I believed that my father was an alcoholic. This is what also deterred me from drinking. If one must drink do it at home when you do not have to drive, etc. visual impairment and road altercations can all be portrayed differently when under the influence of alcohol. This is not my expertise but I do know that the results can be deadly. Mental health problems can lead to a person using alcohol to self-medicate as well as pills and other substances that are mind altering.

Once we left the rooming house we lived in, my mother moved in with her boyfriend. My biological father and mother never lived together while I was in New York. Once he brought me to New York I seldom saw him. My mother provided shelter for me but not a safe haven place. My so called step father, her common law husband, started to sneak in my room at night. He raped me at six years old. Once I began to develop at age 11-12 he began raping me again when my mother was at work. I had never really bonded with my mother, so how could I expose what he was doing to me? I felt she wasn't there for me. I felt that she was uneducated in many senses. People back then denied the fact that a child was never to blame for rape or incest. They were victims, their abusers predators. I became a baby sitter for her which I resented. I could not go out alone; I had to take her kids. This act many parents do. This is wrong. Children need to be allowed to be children. Maybe she thought she was protecting me, traveling with these tella tales. Later I became a surrogate wife to my mother's live in boyfriend. I always wanted to know why men rape children. I suppose that's what led me to work in a psychiatric hospital for 15 years. As I learned, I got on the job therapy, not enough.

My mother worked the evening shift. She was not there to protect me. I don't believe she knew what was going on. As a parent, we must be careful who we live with. I'm not trying to bore you, just explain who I am and why I am who I am. Some of our relationships are good or bad. I became interested in singing because my mother's boyfriend Harold, use to play the blues a lot. I began to sing pouring out my feelings in each word sung. People use to say to me you sing loud, you're not good enough, etc. Most of the time the negative feed-back took its toll on me, who already had a low self-esteem problem. I was robbed of my youth and my pride. I was stripped naked of my worthyness; which left me feeling empty and unfulfilled for many years. I remember singing in the church choir. Though I enjoyed it, I led few songs. The best songs were given to favorites and the more experienced singers. Choir rehearsal was an outlet for me until I accepted a ride from a church member. We had been at a party, not together but as I was about to leave he was leaving. I accepted a ride home. He took a detour down a lonely dark road, no houses. When he stopped the car he started pulling at my clothes. By that age, I was not going to be raped. I pushed him away and scratched him.

I think I was about 17 years old. He soon got the message and took me home. This episode caused some trauma though I told no one. I just stopped going to church for a while. I was feeling more alienated and betrayed.

As I learned to talk about what happened to me as a child I cried less about it. I can remember working at John Hopkins Hospital in Baltimore, MD. I spoke at a conference. They taught me that I wasn't a victim but a survivor. I'll never forget that day. I was so nervous; I could hardly swallow or speak. I took a sip of water with tears in my eyes and told my story. When woman who had never revealed their abuse came forward and spoke, what a feeling for me to hear them exposing their hurt and getting a sense of relief in speaking. This process of speaking about my abuse leads me to many episodes of expressing my feelings. I was getting much needed release of emotional built up. At the age of 54 I emerged as a singer called Dakoda Blue. Dakoda Blue was a name given to me years ago by a patient because I sang the blues, we put the two names together. We know not what tomorrow will bring or even what today holds for us. I realize now that I needed God not a man. God has been with me from the start and I pray that he continues to be with me until the end. Though I am alone, abstinence for 15 years I want a relationship but because of who I am I must have a strong companion. A man that is not overwhelming, but confident, compassionate and understanding with human qualities. A man in touch with God.

As I've side tracked about my dreams I can now pursue them. I was told at a young age that I could not sing the blues and God's songs also. I don't believe this foolishness (hello). The negativity is felt so greatly in many churches. How they continue standing is news to me. So many of our so called spiritual leaders are betraying us. Man can only be a man but when you pick up a bible and so called dedicate your life to the teaching of God have some pride in yourself. You can affect so many, don't lead them astray. We need pure leaders. We have gone through so much as a nation. Betrayal leads to so much unnecessary hurt. Leaders you have needs, when they overpower your godly needs of devotion take a sabbatical. Step by step is a song that I have in my heart, we will make this journey. Yes, I feel that I must make this journey. Letitia, my oldest daughter will be beside me. God Left her here for a big reason. Another song I feel is how much do I owe him. My mother and I used to sing it. I would sing how much do I owe him and my mother would reply oh Lord. Another song is: I woke up this morning with my mind, daddy would sing with his bassey voice. The family would sing, stayed on Jesus. Those down home spirituals that you could feel. Once my dear cousin Tommy died, a spirit died within in our family. We must preserve our spirits they will live on within our hearts. Families don't let your spirit drift. Lift up your heads and open your hearts once again. Let's work together to create a future for our children, sisters, mothers, and friends.

I want to thank my family for being there for me when I needed you, thank you for babysitting, cleaning my house and doing my laundry. For listening to me when I needed to be heard and putting a roof over my head when I needed shelter. Thank you because of you I know so much more. We at times do not say thank you when we should. Sometimes we do not know how. I was put down so low so much that it was hard to accept praise. I would think of a reason to give it up. People would say to me it's ok accepting it. I've been told that I am so much like an angel. I fear to accept this (smile). Fear can prevent us from facing ordinary tasks. Fear can lead us into a decision built not on fact finding. Rushing into a door without first exploring all path ways can cause a lot of harm. We must find a good entrance and know the exits. Know the alternative escape routes and travel your journeys with well thought out interventions. Take wisdom with you and knowledge will follow.

What a feeling, I need a holiday. I'm ready to retire soon and now travel doing God's work. Wind beneath my wings, hero, the Lord will be my wings, because he is my hero. As Mariah, said look into yourself, there is a hero. The tracks of my tears, just one look, songs that I can indeed feel where my tears led me. End of the road. I want to make a difference before I end. Bring it on home to me, Let the good times roll, my children deserve more of me. If you need me call me Lord I need you now, I am calling. As I write many songs are in my heart. You see years ago the words were so important in a song. I'm not too fond of rap music. My problem is I can't hear or understand most of the words spoken. My brain is running on slow they talk so fast. I need not repeat lyrics a thousand times to get the point. Some of us are quick learners. We must be more responsible for our lyrics. We influence the youth of America and abroad. Years ago we got through the depression, with the help of each other. Music was a large factor. Songs enabled us to relieve feelings. We felt the words sometimes relived those moments sung about. Standing on the corner, singing back in those days was therapeutic. Now days, it portrays something different. The moments of yesterday gave us brain food and brain power. We learned from the media and we were fed information from the TV shows. Some emotional shows were able to allow us to cry and vent, therefore relieving some temporary stresses. This allowed us to enter another day. People like tear jerkers. Crying was purgative. But once we release feelings pent-up for years there can be a void if understanding does not follow.

There was a lot of positive influence in the air. For whatever reason negativity is more in the air now. Getting ahead in life is a good thing. As you get yours, extend an appropriate hand when necessary. The public helps entertainers become wealthy. Dollars in the hand is not the only way to assist others. As we cry, watching emotional events on TV, the stress relieved is not enough. My motto: was always know what you are crying for. Unsubstantiated crying can be a sign for the need of professional help. As I have seen much on TV. I realize a bit of harmful traits exposed there. TV Shows that ridicule people can have everlasting effects on ones psyche. Do we have to be detrimental just to say your approach is not good enough or you need more practice? I'm just a nobody trying to tell everybody about somebody who will save everyone; I am talking about God. I would like to be able to help release more positive energy into the atmosphere. God knows there is too much negative influence in the air. We go out with a positive attitude; sure enough a wrench is thrown into your path. If the hit is too hard some of us cannot recover on our own; but we fail to ask for help. We are made up of building blocks as we build them up some children never learn how to stack them. They constantly knock or tear them down creating an unfinished product. We must provide children, the leaders of tomorrow with the proper equipment that will enable them to venture out into today's world with a fighting chance. We must help them not to detour or distract them.

Novemenber 11, 2005 today is my son Paul's birthday. I am 56 years old and he is 13 years old. This year has been so hard; we have grown apart since Letitia's open heart surgery in February 08, 2005. I have become distant. I don't even know myself; gee I'm glad and proud to be able to express my feelings. I'm not ashamed because we must face our shortcomings. As life moves on time seems to stand still. I have not given the other children the attention they deserve or need. Well hey I need attention also. It has been devastating to have a 37 year old daughter who at times now seems like an adolescent. Though her mind is intact her memory fails long and short term. In my daughter's case she was without oxygen for at least 4 minutes. Prior to this event she was a religious sponge, reading as much as she could and praying a lot. She used to fast and pray. I can remember people in need, waiting for her to pray for them. She seemed to have a power with her praying. So realizing that she indeed had risen from the dead pushed me faster to write this book. I felt compelled to show the world God's love and his power. Her response to her traumatic experience having to be retired as a Captain in Corrections at the age of 37 was what work does god have for me to do now. She not once blamed God for what had happened to her. Sure, I was devastated, her sons traumatized but I realized through it she was truly a gift from God. A gift that I had to share with the world. Her recovery had to be sung out. Thank god she's able to walk and talk yet her personality has changed. I love her like I love my other children, but because I am a parent I was thrown into a depression myself. As I cried out for help God has been there for me hearing my midnight pleas. Right now February 08, 2011 a song comes into my heart. This song carried my spirit, relieving my soul of deep torment. Jesus built a fence around me, I've sung that song so many times. The words filled my heart filled my lungs ran through my veins as my heart beat stronger and my chest raised with the emotional outpouring of my stress. The release of my inner turmoil many times. Trying to get a message through to those in need. The words go like this, I wonder if there's anybody here, who lay at midnight shedding crying tears, Lord because they didn't have anyone to help them along the way. And if there is anyone Lord let me tell you what I've done, I ask Jesus to build a fence around me and protect me every day.

I want to put my focus on something different for a minute, please bear with me. You see you need to understand me. This is coming from the mind of a lonely child. As I got older you can understand why the first song I ever wrote was titled, "Please love a lonely girl". But I'm here to say now that my days were not as lonely as I felt back then because truly God has been with me. I'm here to acknowledge that in my lonelist hour God's spirit embraced me giving me the strength to pursue. Giving me the courage not to face another day but face another moment. So you see my story is centered on my faith and my faith has brought me out of a path filled with despair, never breaking my spiritual ties with God. You see people tend to blame God for their short comings and misfortunes. How we are put in certain situations can be debated. Some say, why God let this happen. My focus is how God helps us to get thru situations. This is why I say to people my own quote "if you truly believe in God then you need not worry, ask for his help and believe that your prayers will be answered." So another song comes into my mind. It's a down home song from the South. Your prayers may not be answered when you want them to but they are always right on time,(may not come when you want it, but it's right on time). As we face interruptions, do not let your faith be interrupted. Trust in the Lord with all your heart and soul. You will be delivered in a timely fashion. Sometimes we need to learn through experience. Someone telling you a story does not always get the true message through.

Sanora has helped me through my depression, because it is not a stranger to her. You see Letitia Rice was without oxygen for at least four minutes. When her chest was re-opened and her heart pumped by hand at which time she had a stroke from a clot that was thrown. She was considered clinically dead. Once her heart began to beat I considered this as a rebirth, she was born again. I don't know many people that can say they were brought back from the dead, but indeed my child was raised from the dead. Another song comes to my mind (smile)" he arose, he arose, he arose from the dead." Yes she arises. I lost a child, I went through mourning. At the same time I had to care for her (thank you Lord for getting me through that). I don't know if many people put their focus on my mourning a death. Wow I never had enough time to go through the stages of mourning. I have to laugh now, because in my mind that brings a thought to me that a dear friend that I met in Maryland used to say" child I'm gonna have a nervous breakdown when I get a chance but I just aint got the time." I knew that my mind was being held by a thin string, but I also knew that I could not allow it to break. This is why I constantly pray. You see I talk to God myself. At one time I felt that the preachers were on a higher level than man, and had a more direct contact with God. When Letitia was going thru labor having Hakeem, I chose to go to church rather than go to the hospital when I learned that the cord was wrapped around his neck. I asked the church for assistance in praying for my child and my grandchild. I knew the powers of pray then. Upon reaching home I learned that Hakeem and Letitia were doing well.

It is very trying for someone to answer questions that are asked over and over. Patience, yea quite a bit is what I needed. You see when you've been up all night working a 12 hr shift and you come home to a daughter who needs you, it can be very trying. I prayed for strength. I cried at night when I could there were times when I couldn't. I needed to cry so that as the tears rolled down my cheeks, my body felt much wanted relief. Can I have a cure of my own? We get involved in situations that call for our attention though we ourselves are strained and drained. I constantly ask for God's assistance (and all of his disciples as well). To finish this book, I need quite a bit of help. Thank you Katherine, Antonio and Paul. Please mother Mary help this mother succeed. Please St. Anthony help me find all lost minds and create a way to assist in a world effort to help mend and heal us all. My faith is built on my life experiences shared with God. God has definitely helped me, he has led me and now I pray for strength that I can go out to spread these words of mine, instilled by God. I now know my mission in life it's been a long time coming but as the singer said, "A change is coming". It's a change for me, my children, my family, my friends and those I encounter.

Paul, Hakeem, my mother and Blake and sometimes Dashawn have helped me in caring for Letitia. God please strengthen them; make young men of means and understanding for we have come a long way. Caring for someone at home is a very trying experience. We need more outside help. The government is overwhelmed, we as people must form agencies to help with this typed of care. It is more than us being a sitter, we need trained people. Families where are you?

My son, Paul is so much like his father, who is very quiet and seldom expressed all of his feelings. It's hard to live with someone who keeps you constantly thinking, how does he feel? You see we as people especially women must teach our boys and girls how to have confidence in themselves. We must show them what we do. Lead by example. What is the old theory? "Monkey see monkey do". You smoke and tell your children not to smoke "REALLY?" They see you hitting your spouse or your spouse hitting you, they hear verbal abuse and then you wonder why they become who they are, abusive people. In front of our children we must be guarded and very careful as to what we do and what we say. Children have a habit of mimicking. Right now I think of the farmer and dale. The farmer kicks the wife and the wife kicks the child and the child kicks the cat and the cat eats the rat.

The past few days so much has been in the newspaper about a little girl who was killed by her stepfather, this is the year of 2010. Her mother who was insecure, unwillingly allowed this to occur (not on a conscious level). People who abuse children leave a big question mark in my mind. What was their childhood like? Was this behavior learned? Was it something they saw or something that happened to them? What frame of mind are you in when you hurt a defenseless child? What rage is building in you? There are so many reasons why this can happen. Drugs are known to cause violent behavior. Feening for drugs can put the mind in a state that it will do anything to seek out its craving. Then we have the typical people. The husband over stressed at work, the wife is at home caring for the children (the man the bread winner). He comes home over winded his whole being seeking for release. All he needs is one misplaced word from his wife and a chain reaction begins. Results spousal abuse; also child abuse. Is it not abusive to see your father beat your mother or vise versa?

Let's go back in time I used to feel that my own mother was an angry individual. She had a live-in boyfriend who physically and verbally abused her most of the time. At times when she felt that she had to beat me, I was beat with an extension cord (weapon of yester year). It made welts on my body as it tore my skin. It stung and burned, sometimes bled. I guess she was hurting so much that to inflict pain on me was not so bad if she felt I deserved it. I remember once playing hooky from school (we were only in the park) well another cousin passed by and saw us sitting on the swings. Knowing that we were out of school too early she proceeded home and told on us. My cousin Peggy had a mother who was very gentle, soft spoken. I could imagine her say," now Peggy." My mother was different. I was verbally reprimanded and physically assaulted. The extension cord hit me across my eye. I had a black eye for a couple of days, not a good way to get out of going to school. Trust me; I did not do many things to get a beating. Beatings were not my forte. As a result, I would never hit my children with an extension cord. But as I think back I can remember after learning that my son played hooky, I calmly told him to take a shower. When he finished the shower and was dress I asked him to lie across the bed. I hit him several times on his backside with a belt, enough times for it to sting but not enough to welt. He was put on punishment and I left and went in my room crying for what I had done. I think I hurt myself more than I hurt him. I can say that he is truly my son, because speaking to him from my heart, I can bring tears into his eyes and when this can happen you know indeed you have a true human being. I taught him from a very young age to express himself as much possible, at the appropriate time. I asked for the truth out of him and I would give him understanding. I let him know that we could talk about anything. When he hurts me; I let him know it. As I would tell him tears would come into my eyes and I could see tears come into his eyes. I never wanted him to be ashamed or afraid to cry. If it hurt it hurts. Mentally or physically. My mother had a way with words. Her words were like a sword with a sharp edge. I'd rather she beat me and let it be over with. But with her it was never really over. For the next few weeks every time she saw my face she would rehash the incident. Being constantly compared to other children didn't help my pride or self-esteem. This type of torment can create a type of anger in an individual that will mold into their personality. We even unconsciously do the same deeds to others. Remember part of our behavior is learned. For years I have said that as man we put so much into healing our bodies and so little into healing our minds. Well of course before man can get into someone else's mind he must truly know his own. Who really knows and accepts himself? Can you know yourself to the fullest? Why you do this and why do you do that? We might not answer all of the whys because the mind has ways of protecting itself by blocking out information harmful to itself. We need to use our knowledge to help ourselves and others. This is what I pursue. I want to use my involvement as a psychiatric nurse for over 20 years to help give support to as many minds as I can. My medical experiences of 43 years this is now 2012 will help me to conquer my goals also. Lord help me to strengthen my brain and bring forth energy that I can use to become a leader of man, women and be there for all people. Racial equality is definitely my forerunner. I want to go forth promoting good mental health, good physical health and good spiritual health. At this time in my life I would like to pursue my musical career. Giving me insight into body, mind and soul. Helping me to become a complete person. Through my musical inspirations I will send out vibes pent up in me and waiting to be released. You see I am an emotion singer. Through my life I have put my music on a shelf. During times of stress I find it really hard to sing. You see a strong as I am. I have a flip side I can cry at the drop of a hat. We need to balance ourselves in life, so that anger can never take over completely. We have to learn to deal with anger because it is a very powerful emotion. Anger Management is a science and needs to be taught as a growing up tool. When we say no to a tot and he/she stumps, yells, or falls to the floor we need to see this for what it is. These subtle beginnings are the roots being penetrated into the mind of that child. Recognize and respond. Don't ignore the true signs of temper tantrums. We cannot always prevent them but we can buffer them. As we teach our children that no means no, not maybe. Wait means just that. Children have to be taught patience. As well as we need to adopt some there are times when I know that If I had been a little more patient a problem would have had a different result. When we act impulsively, anxiously we tend to create a manner that will influence the person you are dealing with. Impatience has a power of its own; you tend to push out vibes into the atmosphere creating a faster pulse which creates a quicker thinking response. There are times when we need to act fast and others times when we need to really evaluate our response since it will truly effect another person actions.

You see I've always taught my children to stop a second and think about a situation before entering into it. I try to teach them to not act impulsively, though there are times that we must act immediate to save our lives. I give this example, you get into a heated argument, voices raises, and the person pushes, and you push back. Now the person slaps you, you punch them. So you fight until one person is down and can't get up? I'm sure many incarcerated individuals wish they would've taken a moment to think through a situation. We must learn that walking away can save you for another day. The macho attitude can truly get you killed. In the long run is it worth it, maybe to you, but is it worth it to your family and friends? A child loses a father and mother due to street violence. What a lesson to be learned here? What pictured is stored in this child's mind? Can you understand if years later he pursues the street mentality? A child's mind is very delicate. There are grown-ups who cannot handle death appropriately. Mourning has stages that we must follow in order to continue having a healthy mind. So when a parent is stricken down violently, this situation may keep replaying in a young mind. Truly professional help should be considered strongly. Anyone who has encountered a traumatic experience such as this needs to open up and speak about it. When speaking to someone who is not trained may cause further harm. So you see look at what we can prevent by just walking away. You leave with your life. Are you ready to give it up so quickly over a few words? If so you need to find out why you are suicidal. I've learned that many a depressed people do not have the courage to harm themselves but will truly provoke others to do this deed. I say, I am not going to help kill you. Years ago we as black people were beat down. We were continuously told that white was right. Some of us even passed for white. Those who had the nerve to interact with white females were persecuted, tormented and even hanged. We're talking about the old South. What does it feel like to walk down the street having to step aside for a white person? Not being able to even look them in the eye for fear of retaliation. What psychological trauma was inflicted on many a man of color because of this. Years and years of withdrawn behavior, years of hatred pushed into the subconscious of minds unable to verbalize their feelings. Verbalization could mean punishment, or even death. As I think now in 2011 with my mind, my brain, advanced mentally as I am I wonder if some of these things could be transferred into our DNA. Could this later affect our own children? I don't know? Does anyone know? You can raise a child to be prejuduice but is there a way that we can breed a prejuduice child via DNA. IN the news right now is a case. A young man was shot down in Florida. It was brought to my attention that prejudice may have been the leading cause why a white individual would have shot down an unarmed black teenager. We make excuses but sisters and brothers our world is years behind. We cannot stamp out prejudice but we can stamp out injustice. Until then we people of color really and truly need to stand up and reach out and help one another.*

Let me go off into another tantrum. As black slaves the people were not allowed to read, they were not allowed to gather in groups. Basically they were told what they could do and what they couldn't do by their masters. The master many times raped the women. Sometimes the black female had to nurse the white children though blacks were hated and belittled, it was ok to give white babies breast milk from a black women? This is unbelievable so what was a slave to think? I'm good enough to cook for the master, I'm good enough to watch the Master's children but yet unable to be properly paid for doing the farm chores. The slave helped to maintain the income of the master, but reaped very few benefits. The black man of the South was spit on, pushed, verbally abused over and over. I hear you brothers and sisters of the yester years. No one could have felt your pain. No one could have understood the depth of your torment, had they not been there. But yet when other races rehash their torments you and I, are suppose to so understand. Our story is down played it was ok for crusaders to rip us from our native land? We were ok living in Africa, they had their tribes they had their ways, they had their traditions. You tell me why it's ok that someone from another continent can pull you from your family and rob you of your heritage? Take you from your Mother's breast, hearing mothers crying, sisters and brothers taken going all over the world. Never seeing each other again. Lost sometimes most of the times forever. When do the brethren mean just that? We as people of color need to face up once again and do our part. Stop believing that the government will bail you out (hello). Life liberty and justice for all. When this happens we can all rejoice. Until then we people of color really and truly need to stand up reach out and help another. Right now we are all we have each other in most cases. There are a lot of caring people of non color I don't take credit from them. I acknowledge them ok.

We need good black schools in America. Schools where we can teach our heritage. Did you know that the first open heart surgery was performed by a black man? Why not? For years and years black men have joined white men in progress in our nation. We were right there right alongside the white man. But when the credit is given sometimes there's no mention of the black. Most times we are not even said to have walked behind the white man because for reason it was as if we were invisible. Let's stop being invisible. We know now how our knowledge has done marvelous things to lead up into our future.

January 21, 2006 Letitia and I would like to dedicate our lives to helping the Youth. Sounds big but we want to start with our children, grandchildren and move forward. One child at a time. My hope is built on the Lord. Every time that I hear that someone else that I know has died it reminds me that I have not accomplished what I have set out to do. Be entertainer, educator, teacher promoting a healthy body and mind. I am a Christian who seeks to give hope to those who have forgotten that Christ is alive. I want to give faith to those who have lost or never had faith. I have faith that each of my children Letitia, Sanora, Tycia, and Paul live through their separate ordeals and become leaders amongst their peers. Too many young people follow behind leaders who are lonely sheep themselves. They do steer the youth into doing what they themselves can't, couldn't, or won't do. They brain wash our youth. It is easy to brain wash someone who is lost. Lead someone who has no hope, no faith, and no self-esteem. These people are not always dumb, poor or uneducated. They are simply lost to a cause. They began to follow a cause that may lead to their self-destruction. Many times we get lost in our plans which have no real purpose. This is why I try myself to focus as much as possible. We are all one of God's children so we must not be the cause of the downfall of others.

We as parents try to live out our lives through our children. One subject comes to my mind, child models. Did the parents miss out due to lack of physical endurance or parental assistance? Do not rob your children of their youth to compensate for your short comings. I do agree with parents who expose their children to many options for their future. For instance buy fire trucks, nurses and doctors kits, give them age appropriate computers. Put a spark in their mind. When I read the newspaper and see talk shows I can become more educated on current events. This is why the media can play an important role in conveying a message to the public.

I have to stop a minute and speak about the dress code of today. Young people are wearing the baggy pants pulled below their behind exposing their under wear. What message is being sent out? As people of color we must stand up and start having pride in ourselves. Dropping our pants down, does this mean kiss my ass, smell my ass, I'm confused about the message I'm receiving. Are you sending a coded message? Or are you following the so called leader?! Monkey sees! Monkey do?! The rappers are wearing nice clothes some of their pants are dropped below their waist. Some promote these fashions. They wear their clothes how they chose to wear them. If the youth are protesting against the proper clothing worn on a job who will hire them. As sure as hell they are not hiring each other. Now I'm not having an open war on the dress code of our youth, I'm trying to understand why we are self-destructing. Other nationalities do not have to destroy us because we are doing it to ourselves. There has come a time now that each of us must think alone, as well as be able to collectively collaborate with each other. Stop the hate you can only move forward with a positive attitude. A negative attitude will surly consume you and your dreams. Right now I have to live with the thought that it's not my world I'm just trying to live in it.

We are in trouble folks. Salaries are not going up. Food is higher. Some parents have to pay for their children to go to school on the bus. You pay for them, you pay for you, you buy each of you lunch, and how many pennies do we need a day? What is the message that is given to the poor people now? If you don't have money for a metro card so what if your kid doesn't go to school? Tuitions are higher your kids will not be well educated? Just who are we trying to hold down. An educated man of color is a powerful thing (smile).

As I was watching Ophra, I saw a young lady talking about pornography pictures. When you are broke some people will do anything to eat. When we expose ourselves, exactly what are we thinking and feeling. DO we feel that we have to show more to be liked, noticed, etc. what you see is what you get? Is that true? We are surely seeing too much. What are you giving? Are you offering anything, and at what price? Will this harm your self-esteem, your career, your prestige? People do judge a book by its cover. Years ago the pioneers covered arms and legs. Let's leave something to our imagination in our spouse. A job at McDonald's many times is looked down on. Minimum wage is still a wage. We as young people must realize the need for education. Then on the other hand there's many a people working at McDonald's, K-marts, etc. who have a college degree. Just know that you need to work and provide for yourself as much as possible. I've always admired the people on the street who push a cart full of bottles and cans. They are not taking advantage of another person, they are not pan-handing. They are simply trying to support themselves. I feel for them because of what they have to go through to collect their cans. I don't want to imagine the germs they come in contact with. From the time my son was only 5 or 6 years old, I would pull over to the side of the street and give strangers with bottles 5 dollars. Five dollars might have been more than those 2 big bags of bottles they carried. Five dollars to me was a small amount since we as Americans waste a lot. But those people each and every one in their own language would give me a smile and say God Bless you. Indeed I needed these blessings because for some reason I get charged from helping others.

I have to say this because a thought just came to my mind. It is very annoying to me to see store workers using gloves as they are cutting meat and going to the cash register never removing the gloves. What are they protecting themselves? It's like too many times this happens and they have the nerve to look at you when you complain. Let's put the gloves under the microscope, do we want to know the germ count. Some workers still handle your food without gloves.

Peace on earth good will to all men, white, black, and red, yellow, all. Have we forgotten the March in Washington and what it was about?

Can I sing Hallelujah, the storm is passing over, and I hope the storm will blow out to sea. Let the Sun shine in let the rainbows shine through. Lord Jesus Christ our savior save us from ourselves. We are looking forward to our family reunion this July; there are several family members that will not be there. Members who we love and truly miss. So each reunion has begun to have more meaning to me personally.

As a young parent I allowed my mother to care for my oldest daughter. The school was closer to my mother's house though I lived in the neighborhood. On an unconscious level I was allowing my child to be cared for by someone other than myself as my mother once did to me. I give excuses for my mother helping to raise my daughter I have always loved my daughter but I was not ready for her birth because of this I failed her. Now I have the opportunity to help her. It's about facing up to your short comings, experiences and acknowledging your failures. I failed her severely. She was raped as a teenage because I was wrapped up in myself. I didn't expose the animal who raped us both. She has lost some of her past memories and short term memory but some things might be best forgotten. We all handle stress in different ways.

A few days ago I was so angry with my grandson, but I must remember it is hard for him to show love to his mother. I guess somewhere in his mind he might have been thinking where was she when I needed her. Because of her personality change my daughter is like a stranger to her children and most people. When she was in the hospital she had a blank stare. I almost wanted to say, as I looked into her eyes, Letitia are you there? As time went on her eyes cleared up and each day, each month and each year; I could see her spirit returning. My grandson was in pursuit of some forbidden fruit. He was into a lot of negative behavior that caused a lot of emotional turmoil in the house. Though his friends never directly disrespected me coming into our house and being in his company as he blasted the music was indeed a form of disrespect. When you see that someone is doing wrong and you're in their presence I can't see you as the innocent by stander. There were times when my grandson would verbally abuse me in front of his friends. Though I stood up to him in front of them I would retreat into my room in solitary despair. I cried many a nights for God to please intervene. There were times when I would find myself yelling as loud as he was yelling. The aftermath of which I had a rapid pulse and an overwhelmed mind. There were times I went to work without any sleep because he would be playing music so loud. My thoughts were truly not my own. Sometimes we have to download and at those times when I would share some of this information, people would say kick him out. That's easy for some to say, but truly there were times that I was afraid of him though I held a firm front. You see many young people today use a drug called ecstasy, it may give them elevated highs but if in an angry state it will elevate the anger and distort the whole picture. There were times when I spoke to him and he would get angry literally foaming at the mouth. So you see there was fear in my heart, fear that I believed well justified. Young people of today, let me speak to you for a minute, stop intimidating your family, stop showing off in front of your friends, you are only fooling yourself. You need your family more than you realize. If you have no job, if you don't have an apartment, what really belongs to you? How many services is your family providing for you? So treat them with kindness and respect. For you are indeed the one with the problem. Man up, face up and do something about it. I thank God that in the year of 2010 my grandson went to college. Thank you Jesus, thank you Lord for answering my prayers. There were times when I prayed and I knew that it might take a while but my prayers would be answered. This is why I say to you, I truly believe in God. At the height of my emotions as I prayed that God would prevent me from having a heart attack or a stroke, I was delivered into calmness.

As i think back to Letitia coming home from the hospital I can remember her constantly saying how come no one is visiting me. Well there are two answers to this question. We as people use excuse to stay away from situations that make us uncomfortable. Illness is surly one of these instances. I truly can understand this. To see a loved one who was so promising become so severely misplaced can indeed interrupt our own equilibrium. Life is truly a struggle for most and to face a depressing situation for many cannot tolerate. Yesterday a person jumped off the Brooklyn Bridge, September 2010. Another person jumped off the Staten Island ferry boat. Times are hard and painful. We must look up for answers from God. Looking down and depressed is a road dangerously ridden. We expose ourselves too much that can happen to us when we don't focus our attention on our surroundings. Please Lord help me to make a difference; one life at a time. Please multiply this experience as I grow. I have grown, I have weltered but I am in full blossom now. I am learning my place. I have yet to be placed there. But with the help of God and others I pray to succeed.

I must not forget the experience I had while I sat in the hospital, when my oldest daughter was in critical condition. Prior to Letitia's surgery we had been joking around at home. I had a teddy bear that was now a little rugged. I had no one else to hug intimately so I slept hugging the bear. When Letitia went into surgery to my surprise my cousin Bam went down to her car and brought back a large cuddly teddy bear. Letitia had told her to give it to me while I waited for her to have her surgery. I didn't realize then that it was to become my soul mate while I was in the hospital. Once I realized that Letitia's heart had stopped in the hospital minutes after reaching the CCU from recovery room. I knew that my faith would be the thing to pull us through. She was a spiritual being and now while she laid unconscious I needed to pull on my faith to guide her critical course. I remember telling my cousin Bam who became emotionally overwhelmed when we were given the news. Being me (yea, that's who I am) I told her in a matter of fact statement, Bam if you can't pull it together I will call someone to come and get you. We need to focus on a prayer visual for Letitia. After the doctor explained her condition to me. I asked permission to do what I do best. Bam and I entered the CCU and out of the flow of traffic and directly in front of her bed. We kneeled and prayed. As passerby's observed they first thought that I had collapsed they soon realized I was praying. I met many people on that unit. I prayed with many families for my loved one and their loved ones. I even met a nurse who had worked in one of the hospitals I had worked in (small world). Many people visited my daughter, family, friends and coworkers. I would tell them to please go to her bedside with a positive attitude. Leave the crying at the door. I wanted her to hear hope in their voices. I even had a preacher pray in silence. I don't know what people thought of me but that wasn't on my mind. My child's care was a first and last thing on my mind. The first few days while in the hospital, I saw a vision of Jesus while sitting in the waiting room. I used to look out the window and pray at night. I had refused to leave the hospital until my daughter's recover. She was on a respirator and was unable to talk. I wanted her to be able to communicate her needs before I left. We as relatives of a patient must feel completely secure when we leave them in the care of medical staff. The medical staff must realize that our confidence in them is important. This is why you do not fuss or argue with someone caring for your needy one. People have a tendency to be vengeful. A sick person doesn't need this. The vision I saw of Jesus was of him standing in the window fully robed. Crown on his head. This gave me a sense of warmth and comfort. A feeling that everything would be alright. I no longer felt alone at night as I stood guard over my child. I also met a security guard that comforted me. He gave me that final push that enabled me to fight the fight. This was February 2008. You see I was fighting for my child's recovery. For whatever reason, she was in critical condition. I knew that Jesus Christ Our Lord was her Savior. This particular guard resembled my grandfather. Speaking to him made me at ease. We spoke each night that he was on duty. He encouraged me not to give up. So with his kind words and familiar face I endured. I pulled more and more on my faith. I slept an hour or two at a time holding my teddy bear feeling close to my daughter. I felt that being there was generating a spirit of harmony for her body that now needed a sense of calm, a sense of peace. She needed to know that I was near. I constantly told her this. Lord God I learned a lot then and now. I would sing spirituals to Letita. Pouring my heart and spirit into their words soothing her and cleansing me. Though she was gravely ill, I never once let it enter into my mind that she would die. God had brought her back from the brink of death. I knew that there was a purpose in this. I would never blame God for I know that this was not his mission. We live here on earth following a path of our own accord. We must sometimes reap what we sow we want to feel that we can be forgiven for our sins. Is that not why Catholics go to confession. I've confessed to God directly. Asking for help to overcome and over power the evils of this world. When Letitia awakened from her coma, she told me that she had seen Jesus Christ. I truly believe her. So she was sent back here to teach people the work that God can do and has done. She is truly raised from the dead.

Thinking back in time about my first born Letitia. I could remember back when she was a teenage when I didn't know how to hug her, when she was crying. I did not know how to approach her. Wow, I remember I failed to tell her I loved her as many times as I should have. We as parents must be able to hug our children and tell them we love them. This will enable them to pass it on to their children. When I think back it's hard to remember my mother hugging me and telling me she loved me. So I tried to break the cycle, so now most people that I know and feel dear to me I tell them I love them. They may not understand me and why I say this. But I truly say it with meaning and feeling. I love you quote I love your spirit. I love you, I love the way you make me feel when I'm with you. Love crosses many boundaries. Breaks down many walls. I truly have the love of people in my heart. Why else would I have given my life to my nursing career nurturing people as best as I could? Now I tell Letitia all the time that I love her. We joke around a lot and one day I said to her as I was giving her a ring for her birthday, I love you will you marry me. She said, to me thank you for being my mother and thank you for standing by me when I was in the hospital. She said to me will you take care of me for the rest of your life? Of course I said yes because this truly one of my goals. So you see after many years of holding in my feelings as best I could I try now to release them. In life most people do not feel comfortable with a person as straight forward as myself. But I truly am the type of person that can say what I need to say to you to your face. Speaking behind someone's back can truly cause a lot of problems. The message can never be accurate. Some of our memories are not accurate. So when the story is heard a second time there's usually words added which could completely change the meaning of what was told or what was said. Sometimes words are depleted conveying a new or different message on purpose.

I'd like to change the flavor of my conversation briefly. I worked in a hospital as a registered nurse because of longivity on the job, many times I was placed in a charge position. My duties consist of being responsible for the people working that given night. My interpretation is I'm the fall guy. At work some workers act out their anger on others and me. They enter the building carrying the weight of their day's activity. It's a job that is very trying you see some patients are also inappropriate. We need to realize that people in general have heightened emotions when they're sick. We try to give the best care we can under these circumstances. As staff we have to be able to take verbal abuse and do our jobs. When a person is hurting immobile, and unable to do their daily routine their temperament can change. On the other hand some people are just plain mean. Their attitude is not going to change because they came into the hospital. Some employees have personality deficits that they carry with them where ever they go. We as a nation must learn to deal with our problems. It takes skills to deal with anger especially when we were never taught how. Strike out is what most people do, tit for tat, hit for hit, who turns the other check these days? This is why problem solvers should be part of every job there are small and larger problems but all need to be thought out not swept under the rug. There are times when staff needs to sit at a round table and collectively discuss a problem. Now days the government is trying to pass a law to prevent work place bulling. I heard it on the news 11/12/11. I could remember in nursing school we had a patient name Mrs. Reynolds. She was one of the worst patients you could image. She always had her finger on the call bell. When you entered the room it was hard to leave, for she held you hostage in conversation. She took up so much staff minutes that the team needed to respond to her behavior. As a result of group discussion the team realized that Mrs. Reynolds was simply lonely and afraid. How this problem was solved was that staff members began to periodically go into her room uncalled. They would simply come in and say hello Mrs. Reynolds how are you doing? Or they would just come in to say I'm just checking on you I'll be back. They learned to take turns causing one person to be less overwhelmed. Mrs. Reynolds was afraid of the night, so she didn't sleep well. There are a lot of people in the hospital for some reason has a hard time sleeping at night. As a psychiatric nurse I knew working in a psych hospital exposed me to many patients wondering around during the wee hours of the night. I learned how to deal with them. Dealing would sometimes mean sitting and talking to them for a few minutes. Quietly singing to them and more on a medical hospital setting I would simply hold their hand. The reason that I am saying this is because we need to be careful touching psychiatric patients. A psychiatric person has an aura around them that they will protect even strike out if this barrier is crossed. Some are pushed needlessly. We meet so called "crazy" people in life. They do not wear labels letting us know who they are. So be careful who you touch. Crazy is a label that I don't like, disturbed is more appropriate. Students today have a great deal of internal conflicts. Some are pushed needlessly; I felt that at times I had college teachers whose goals were to keep some students down. We need to stop this behavior. A degree does not give any one ammunition to badger a young mind. We must realize that teacher's professionals, all human beings are prone to some type of behavior that can be the down fall to another. We must safe guard not ignore the symptoms as they unfold. Do not allow inappropriate behavior to go on where it can be seen and corrected. Stop turning the other cheek (assuming well it's not happening to me or anyone I know).We truly need more accountability in this world of advancement. If one reflects too much on the past events it can truly effect or damage your future.

As black people we share one thing in common (some of us). We have the skill to make others laugh about our life experiences. They can be very funny though at the time we were going through them it can be very sad. Let's turn to another direction for a minute. Violence in the work place is truly on the upscale now that the economy is at its lowest. For some people work has become one outlet for their release of stress. Our leaders, supervisors, need to be more educated on how to handle employee problems. They need to seek out help via seminars and other staff relationship course. They must learn how to deal with stress on the job and know when more professional help is needed.

Sometimes we as supervisors get caught up in a power struggle that does not provide an outlet for solution. The problem gets even more complicated when we talk about race differences. I know that colored folk by history get a little warm blooded with certain high energy conversation. We must concentrate on keeping a low calm voice. We have to set the stage for a productive outcome. So what does the non-person of color do? Sometime they intimidate us (maybe on purpose) pushing our blood pressure up. Shifting the attitude at times. Let's stop the nonese too many violent situations can be prevented or defused. Speaking to a disgrumpled worker needs thought. Do not wait for the last straw to be broken. And do not be the last person to break the straw. We need sensitive leaders. We need psychologically trained staff on each job site troubleshooting (I qualify want to give me a job?) a boss who ignores the cries of workers, who think that a problem is trivial is very insensitive. Any problem quote trivial or major can have a strong impact to the person dealing with it. One person's problem can become many souls reactive and collective downfall. When we work with people we must have a positive mind. Whether we work in Kmart, McDonalds, or a hospital. Treating people with respect and kindness should be your forerunner. You cannot know what troubled baggage one carries with them.

An event came up several years ago as I was working in a psychiatric hospital. I also worked private duty and at this time I was taking care of elderly gentlemen. I had finished my duties at 11pm and as usual before I left the room I would touch my patient's hand. I would usually do this before departing. This particular night I realized his hand was a little warmer than usual. As a nurse, we begin to learn the feel of an elevated temperature. So I took his temperature. It was approximately 99 degrees. Nothing to write home about but I felt that it was on its way up. As I gave my report to the nurse coming in, I made a point of letting her know this information. As I got home that night I thought to myself I wonder if his temperature was elevating. So the next day, naturally I said to my patient how was his night? He began to tell me about a dream that he had had. From the moment that he started explaining the dream, I became mesmerized. My attention now focused only on his voice. He was my center of attention (my undivided attention) He said to me, the president got shot. At that time Ronald Reagan was in office. As they say my ears began to stand at attention. My throat became tight; my respirations began to deepen my equilibrium becoming unbalanced. He had my full attention and heightened emotions. As I think back I don't remember if this was before he was actually shot or not. Right away I jumped to the point. Did he survive? Oh yea, he said. He was on a plane but his wound was not life threatening. Well for someone else this might have been a simple dream but for me it was a story that began to compel me. I've always been a jump start type of person, once something would start to click, I would move forward with an action. Right away something came into my mind. I felt I needed to convey this dream to higher authorities. Another thought flew through my mind. If you do that they are going to realize after investigating you that you've never filed an income tax return. So I felt that the IRS would be after me. I have worked two or more jobs all of my life so I have indeed paid taxes. But I failed to file. I kept saying I'll do it next year. As the years went on truly I was decades behind. I will get into work situations later on. This was a tough decision to make. One that I never regretted. I decided that on my supper break, I needed to go home because it was only blocks away and make a few phone calls. I believe I first called the CIA getting the number from the operator. After a few minutes I was cut off. Of course not until I stated who I was my address and my phone number. Now all of the sudden my phone would not work. Me being the intelligent person that I am knew that something was up and out of my control. I had a cousin that lived nearby so I decided to go to her house to use her phone. Once again, I was cut off after a few minutes. Then I remembered her daughter had a separate line. So I decided to use a different technique. I can't remember where I got this information. But I do recall hearing that if someone wanted to speak in the White House it was possible. So this time I asked the local operator to connect me with the Washington DC Operator. She answered with her southern drawl can I help you? As I was connected I became a person in a Trans like state. I explained with urgency in my voice that I needed my message conveyed to the secret service, the people taking care of the President. I could bet my boots that this conversation was monitored. I was crying, shaking, and very sincere as I told my story. As I ended my conversation, I said to her please see to it that my message be conveyed to protect the President. After I went back to work that evening since I was only on a break, I was immediately called down to the nursing office. The supervisor was present and I believe the two suited men were from the CIA. They introduced themselves and I began telling my story (my patient's story) one of the men looked me straight in the eye and said to me a little snotty, what do you think that you are? A clairvoyant? I just looked at him making direct eye contact now becoming a little teary eyed and with sincerity in my heart, I said to him, Can you tell me for sure that this isn't going to happen? He didn't continue with his statement. Well needless to say, I was sent home (Nurse gone mad). That night (since I worked two jobs) I went to work at a local psychiatric hospital to my surprise two other nurses were on duty. Never before had I worked with two other nurses. But it didn't take a genius to know that the hospital was trying to make sure that I was safe enough to care for the patients. Well I guess I passed the test because later on I worked with only one nurse as usual. For a period of time I know that my phone was tapped. It became annoying after a while. When speaking on the phone I felt as if I was in a vacuum an echo chamber, a telephone booth. I knew that to make a statement that I had made would cause me to be investigated. Realizing this I still moved forward to expose my patients dream. After that someone was showing pictures around my neighborhood of me because a store owner told me. I have learned in life that when I have feelings about a certain subject I must peruse my ideals. I believe the next day a president of another country was assassinated. Later that week an updated security plan was publicized for our president (coincident?).

This brings me to another incident I remember when my Aunt Honey died. My mother used to go to her house for a couple of hours to help her daughter care for her at home. She was bedbound and needed total care. The family members took turns helping. Sometimes my mother wanted me to go with her and I would assist if I could. One particular night Aunt Honey seemed to be in much distress. As I entered her room I knew that she was in her last days. Not realizing then that this was her last day. Aunt Honey had raised my oldest brother, who is younger than me. She had cared for him when my mother was young and working in New York. Aunt Honey lived in the South at that time. When my mother wanted to care for my brother herself Aunt Honey refused to give him up. Well I can understand that he was like her child. She had been with him through his younger years, the years that were so important to a child's development. As Aunt Honey became increasingly restless sitting at her bedside and holding her hand, I said to her, Aunt Honey its ok you can let go we all love you and we know that you love God. We know that you've had a relationship with God and you need not fear leaving this world because there's no doubt in my mind that you won't be with God. From a young age I've been able to accept death as a part of the living mechanism (can I say that we are born to die) well little did I know that as I sat besides her holding her hand that Aunt Honey would take her last breath. At that time a strange sensation was felt in my hand. I felt something entering my hand. Don't ask me to explain this just take my word for it. As we went to Aunt Honey's funeral I can remember sitting in the church and feeling a compulsion to stand up. For whatever reason I felt that I needed to speak to my family on behalf of Aunt Honey. I felt that I was truly to give them a message. At that time in my life, I wasn't as secure with myself as I am now. So I didn't get up and relay the message that I had felt in my heart. I was supposed to say that Aunt Honey wanted her family to love one another. Later I told this to my aunt Mert. We lived distances apart but I've always felt very close to her. Indeed I felt that she understood me. Indeed I felt that she understood my madness because I believed that some of my relatives thought of me as being the crazy one. I don't know if crazy is the correct word but they truly felt that I was overly emotional. They knew that as we sang together as a family I would always want to sing songs that would bring tears to your eyes. Songs for example, will the circle be unbroken, which tells of a mother being carried in Hurst and the question will her survivors continue their circle of love. I regretted the fact that I didn't stand up in the church and give that message and to my surprise her obituary paper stated the word love. Exactly what I was to tell my family. Well my aunt Mert told me that I should tell them anyway but I did tell a few people at different times but not when I should've when we were all together. So you see by history I have held in words that should've been spoken so now I was breaking that cycle. This is one of the reason I speak my mind whenever possible. Last words could affect an outcome of any situation. This brings to mind my father's funeral. My father had not seen me for over 20 years when he called me. One of his sisters worked where I worked so she probably gave him my number since I was usually in contact with her. My father stated to me I'd like for you to come visit me I am in the hospital in South Carolina. His voice sounded very weak. His speech was pressured. After hanging up I thought to myself he's dying. Being young as I was in those days, I wasnt responsible enough to put myself on a plane and go to see him. I had thought to myself I haven't seen him for years. And now he wants me to jump up and come to see him? How insensitive of me. Do I need to tell you that before I made arrangements to see him the next week he had died? This left a void in my life that I could never fill. Did he have something to tell me? I'll never know. I flew to South Carolina on the plane for the 1st time. I had to stop in North Carolina and get on a 2nd plane. Well the 1st flight left me thinking not scared but thinking. You are an idiot for getting on this plane and getting scared. So calm yourself down. There's only two ways to get off land or crash. So I sat back and prayed. As I arrived at the church upon entering I saw the Mortician standing in the back of the church she was a tall good looking woman. Well dressed manicured nails. Hair in style. I approached her saying, this is my father would I be able to sing just one short song? She looked me in the face, and I can still remember her cold stare. She said, I'm sorry but we are running late. So I did the chicken route and jerked my neck back. Saying to myself really? So I sat down in the front and as she closed the casket I sprung to my feet. I walked up to the casket feeling a little overwhelmed and leaned my hand on the casket. I said I flew down here to SC for the first time on the plane and I have to sing this song. I poured my heart into singing Jesus build a fence around me. I rocked the church; I knew this and was told by many. It was not an audition. Just a poor lonely daughter singing to her father. Trying to release all the guilt pent up feelings that I had in me at that time. As a mortician I feel that you have a responsibility not only to the deceased but to the living. The treatment rendered at times like these can influence the grieving process. If one can lay their loved one down with a feeling of warmth and security this will probably be a catalyst leading to a peaceful calm that is so much needed at this time. My aunt (my father's sister) later told me you are truly your father's daughter. Though my father was only five feet (and that's stretching it), he had the character of a 6 foot man. He had confidence in himself. Though he was an alcoholic I felt that he had a way about him. This type of aura made others want to be around him. I feel that I inherited this charisma. Those around me have as much fun as I do. I like to be happy, loving and funny. Dig it and jive turkey, were part of my father's rap. Hey Maaaan what's happenin still rings in my ears. Words that was sacred to him. He was truly a smooth talker. So you see I have tried to lead a path now, where as I must stand up for what I believe in. I am not trying to hurt anyone's feelings, but I am indeed trying to protect my own. This made me who I am as far as expressing what I feel I need to tell others. This led me into a journey of inspection. Observing how people, who feel the power, can control another person's destiny. Just because you choose a profession, as a mortician does not give you the right to treat the living unkindly. It's not about you. You are giving a service to the living on behalf of the deceased. This made me check out myself, I vowed to say what I needed to say to a person while they were breathing. Do not wait until tomorrow because we cannot always predict a person's death. I do not know till this day if he had something to tell me. Praise those you love while they can hear the praise. Just like give me my flowers while I can smell them see them touch them. Speak with kindness of me so that I can hear it. You can't soup me up at my funeral. Another death that affected me was when my so called step-father/rapist died. This was 20 years ago, now I had already told my mother before I moved to Maryland that he had raped me and Letitia. She seems skeptical. I don't know if she ever believed me. Well anyway, I thought that she had to be out of her mind to ask me to go to the hospital with her to care for him as he was dying. Never the less I went. I had just moved back to New York from Maryland; a relationship gone badly. My mother would change his diapers and I would hold him over turning my head. He was dying of Cancer. I thought how could she ask me to do this? She cares about him so much and me so little. When he died I had ambivalent feelings about his death. I was glad that the monster who changed my whole life, invaded my daughter's sanity was no longer breathing. Then on the other hand, I was ashamed to feel this way because when he was sober he was caring, he portrayed a different picture. I did feel some relief as I spoke with my daughter and could see a healing process taking place. My daughter said to me that what he had done to us imbedded in our spirit, but God would see us through.

I was once harassed on a job I had. I had witnessed patient abuse. There had been other staff members there, and we were sick of seeing this black youth being abused by a white staff member. You see we talked about how wrong it was for this to happen. We talked about exposing this but none of us had the courage to begin the process. One evening, I was in charge as usual and I again witnessed this abuse. Yes the kid was bad and always starting trouble. This particular day he had to be put in restraints. As far as I was concerned he was also abused at this time. The staff member would use what is called excessive force, you know twist an arm harder than necessary; put his knee in to the kid's chest. We all felt the kid's pain and one day it was more than I could handle. So I decided that without telling anyone else; that I was going to report this to New York State commission of the Mental Health. I preferred to travel to Manhattan to do this. Wellbeing so called of sound mind, I realize that I needed to think this over clearly. Well you know, I knew that a witness probably would not come forward. So after a few sleepless nights I decided I would go alone. I prayed and asked God for the strength because I knew this move would change my life, not knowing to what extent. I had enough scruples to know that I was not going to report this to Staten Island, afraid it was going to be swept under the rug and that I would be fired. I made an appointment and was interviewed. At the interview I brought some pictures with me and showed them. I was told to go back to Staten Island, and report this at the facility that I worked in. Once I put this in writing my whole world changed. Can I say it ended in a way? I have never since had so much abuse thrown at me. I look back at reading and seeing movies about prejudice but now I was getting a front row seat. To see what happens when a poor black goes up against some white middle class bigots. My team leader and her disciples made my life miserable. You know the kind of things that you feel and other people see but you can't control nor prove it. Well listen up here she was not so untainted herself. She would have staff parties where she was sexually provocative. Well this wasn't the worst thing that had happened at a party that I had gone to. At one party some white people came into the room wearing paper white hats and carrying a lit white candle. Never in my wildest dream have I been prejudice. I grew up babysitting for a white family, so I was used to being around white people and they treated me with the upmost kindness. I now felt like an innocent victim. They knew about my sexual abuse because I had learned to speak about it, my rape and molestation. I would over hear the white staff talking out loud saying things that were mentally damaging to me. There were many days that I would run into the bathroom and cry. I would wash the tears away. I was not always able to clear my eyes because they were red or my face was flushed. Now I was the abused one. Coming to work barley able to relax. Feeling on edge and tensed all the time. Trying my best to hold my emotions together in a place where emotions spilled over all the time. Doing my best to relate and interact with the patients there for treatment. Boy could I have used some. As I spoke with patients I remember sometimes feeling my eyes fill up with tears. They thought I was feeling their pain they never knew my torment, one I could not reveal. How could I say that the team leader, acting supervisor and therapy aids had me on their hit list. They were coming to work to enjoy bullying me, humiliating me and degrading me. How could I have been so dumb changing my whole life, my whole being for a young black man I really didn't know? God knows I hurt but indeed I knew I had done the right thing and I was not going to back down. These are the tactics that people use on the so called whistle blowers. People who can no longer live with the guilt of knowing that something is wrong in a system. But who protects Us? They are ridiculed. Some of those lashing out know that the deeds disclosed are wrong. They fail to stand up because sometimes you stand alone. Alone to man but to me I will always be standing with God on my side. We must have the courage to do what's right. Don't let a few disrupt the majority. At this party all the blacks that were present looked at each other, I believe we were all thinking the same thing and we later discussed it, the KKK here in New York? Staten Island, NY? How dare them. I can't even remember the purpose of this stunt was but I do know that I took pictures of this event and showed them later to the Commissioner of Mental health in Manhattan. I could see that some of them were actually shocked, shocked that the staff could have been stupid and be photographed. I now had evidence. I even called the NAACP. But I backed down because I didn't want this to down play the patient abuse. I knew that for years this place that I worked in was most lily white. They had a society that most employees were either friends or relatives. I was hired because of a friend who knew a team leader. After reporting my harassment I asked to be placed on another unit. I felt that my career as a nurse was threatened. I could no longer work on that unit, crying and feeling humiliated daily. So I was finally placed on another unit and the committee finished their investigation. They slapped the staff on the wrist having them attend affirmative action meetings. Well enough of that because a lot of pain has been resurfaced restored in my life. I felt betrayed because no other staff member stood with me. I realized that they were all afraid for their jobs. So I understand the meaning behind their silence. I truly do. I feel no anger toward them I'm [proud of myself. Proud of Patricia Boyd, the Nurse. The only person with the courage to expose horrible actions toward a mentally ill patient. As I think back other events came up while I was working in psychiatry. One night I was on duty and had taken my break I was working the night shift. I had gone off the unit and was sitting with my feet up in a designated break area. Well needless to say I fell asleep briefly. I was dreaming I was inside a bar not far from the job. I was observing a scene not really part of it. Two people were injured, I believe one died. The other person had injuries non-life threatening. There had been a fight. I could see that the weapon used was not a knife. I then awakened feeling that this was weird. The next morning at 7:30 am as I was going home, I told a friend of mine who was driving home about what had happened. I had also told the nurse that was working with me that night. To my surprise that evening the same story appeared in a local news paper. My interpretation of this is that I had had an out of the body experience. Weird things have happened to me all of my life. I went to Brooklyn to get amniocentesis. This test was done by inserting a needle into my pregnant abdomen to with draw fluid from the sack that the embryo was in, prior to that an ultra sound was done. The technician said to me, you're going to have a boy. And maybe he'll be a preacher. He's kneeling with both hands together as if praying. Well about a half hour later as we were about to exit Brooklyn we were stopped at a light prior to the bridge. My friend drove me because at that time I didn't drive. We suddenly heard a loud bang as we looked beyond her car across the intersection we noticed a car flying through the air with the greatest ease. As it seemed to be coming directly into our path into her windshield I turned to my right both hands covering my face and cried out Oh my God. By standers would later tell us that the car suddenly turned in the midair landing to the right of her car. I exited the car wanting to stand on some ground.

Once standing I felt safe. I smile when I tell this story each time. Because I say that my son was praying for me. We are very close too much alike but close.

I can remember my aunt Bae used to talk to the "Hanks" is what she called them. Some say she went crazy after my uncle left her. Some say that she had a miscarriage and went berserk regardless, I still loved her. She fascinated me. She used to sit and pick on the guitar. Her husband had been a member of a group many years before. Things happen in our lives that we are afraid to put labels on because they go unexplained. The elderly experienced many strange happenings mostly because of the strangeness they reveal seldom. In the old days back then when electricity was very scarce. Ghosts were rumored to walk around a lot. When my so called step-father died my mother used to feel him sitting on the bed next to her. Strange things occurred in that house. One person died in the house. I remember Blake, my sister Vanessa and I were talking about the witch riding you. Of course my explanation was that you were dreaming. Well we discussed this and to my surprise that same night I fell asleep awaking not being able to sit up. I could not move or scream. I was terrified. Finally it seemed like minutes I thought MY GOD and the spell like feeling was gone. I told my mother about it and she said to sleep with a bible on me. I wore a shirt with a pocket to put the bible in my pocket when I slept. I used to work at Sea view hospital and Nursing Home. There after working into the wee hours of the night I saw what we call an apparition as I was sitting in the room. We could not nap there. This was a room with a TV and a piano. As I proceed to sit on the couch, I noticed the lady coming toward me. I said to myself what is she doing up. As I stared at her silently she disappeared within feet's of me. She was white with long grey hair pulled back into a bun. She had on a long form fitting blue dress with white daisies in the print. I spoke to the other staff members about it and was told that there had been many sightings of people or should I say Ghosts there. It's usual but I never felt threatened or scared just stunned.

Once I dreamed about my cousin Teddy dying and as I walked up to the casket the body was of a light skinned person, Teddy was a darker complexion. The next day I heard that Teddy's light skinned brother had died. Now I was so uncomfortable that I chose not to attend the funeral. My daughter Tycia dreamed of someone stabbing people on the Staten Island Ferry; a few days before it happened. Co-incident (Yea).

Well Colleagues at the psychiatric Center used my own abuse that I experienced and what I had said against me. I once heard them calling me a manic depressive with a split personality. They could have been right but they were wrong to use it against me. Was it right of them to use my downfall to assassinate my character? I was humiliated (as I write about it my throat gets tight and tears come into my eyes). I'm ashamed to say that so called mental health workers could use such mind altercating tactics and deceit. Let me talk about one of my brothers, Blake. I had three brothers but Blake and I had a special relationship. I used to financially support him from time to time. I don't mean pay his rent (since he was squandering off my mother until he died, she was in her 70's and he still didn't have a paycheck) He was on social security for two months before he died. I used to constantly say to him get a job or try to get on social security. He would constantly ask for money. The first check that he got enabled him to get so high that he had a seizure. He was not used to having a large amount of money in his hand at one time. The next couple of weeks he was walking around the house preaching from the bible. That boy knew a lot about the bible. There was a time when he was incarcerated and I believe this led him to become an avid reader. My daughter says that he was her favorite uncle. I never knew that until after his death. I knew that he had some great moments. He was funny at times, I always said that if I had gotten my career in music started he would have been my stand-up comedian (if I could keep him sober enough) he drank beer each and every day and used heroine most of his adult life. He had worked I believe less than 5 years of his entire life but for different things that we needed of him he was there to give us a helping hand. He took care of my daughter Sanora after she was hit by a car in Schenectady, NY. He stayed at night with Letitia after her open heart surgery/Stroke. He took the kids to football practice sometimes he would babysit the boys though he would sometimes sneak out; I'm telling you that our family have been through so much together. Blake could talk a lot sometimes he would procrastinate. That's why I want to get off my butt and write this book and stop my procrastination. I can't hit the lottery so I guess I'll have to use my own resources. I promised God to expose the miracles in my life; that have brought my three daughters back to health. I believe that we need to give back and share information that we learn. Grandparents do this all the time. They can be a source of so much information, not just baby sitters. Sometimes we go through life doing things that amount to nothing, just wondering through life. I let my rape and molestation rule my life in my younger years. I now want to consciously take charge of my life. I know the direction I want to travel. As I go forth I will constantly ask the Lord for a push and for his help and courage. It takes courage to venture out into a world full of man and woman eaters. I had a very good friend who was such an inspiration to me. I used to call her Cold Casion because she loved the cold weather and she was also Caucasian. We had a sister relationship revealing to each other our inner most feelings, this was just like having a psychiatrist. We all need to be able to express our feelings so that we can move on. First we must be man or women enough to take credit for our actions, embarrassing or not. We can put on a plastic smile but true scholars know the difference between what is real and what is not. When we have a true friend that we share our feelings with we must protect his or her privacy. Gossipers make poor friends. They have an eternal pledge to spread the word, your word. A good friend is also a good listener. Sometimes I just needed to bounce my words off of someone. Many times I could figure out my shortcomings, answer my own questions. My best friend Joyce was truly an inspiration to me. She told me like it was. As we had discussions we spoke with love and honesty. We never tried to hurt each other feeling; just make each other aware of them. We were good together. I lacked some skills at times that made my life harder to live. She would explain the situation coming from a different prospective. We need this type of input looking at a picture from different focuses, opening up a new idea leading to a better resolution. This is what our friendship was about. Analyzing information presented and using our own abilities as psych nurses to dig beneath the surface exposing harmful lingering tensions. We coined the phrase that we were only big boys and big girls. Age does not mean maturity. My mind is not as mature as my body. Disruptions in my mental development have caused my mind to fall behind in its maturity. March 17, 2006 who am I? Today is truly the first day of the rest of my life. I had chest pains a couple of days ago. I've been over doing it trying to care for my children and grandchildren, working overtime. I was working three jobs, nurse, parent and grandparent. Well when I had the chest pains radiating down my left arm and making it numb, I realized as I thought to myself you could die you know. I stopped doing overtime (began to live off a lower budget) hard to do. I started to concentrate more on writing my book. I got my strength from God through my daily prayers. Because of the way my life has unfolded sometimes I find it very hard to be physically compassionate. After breaking up with my son's father I find it hard to hug my son or any one. When he hugs me I have to put a time limit on it. Lately hugging has given me a smothering feeling so I pull away. One thing I can't stand is if I'm having a controversial conversation don't try to end it with a hug. If I decide to walk away I feel intimidated if someone tries to hug me to keep me in that spot. I have grown to realize this is truly a problem. I am working on it and have been working on it. If we don't give our children the appropriate touch they will defiantly get it someplace else. Good example when Letita was in the hospital 6 years ago her 13 year old son was devastated. We had become very close because she worked the swing shift in corrections, she was a Captain. Since I lived down stairs I was the baby sitter. I had become closer to both of her sons. At the time Letitia was in the hospital I must say the boys were neglected. Though there were relatives reaching out they truly didn't have any one as close as I had been with them. Both of her sons fathered children. One son was only 13 years old when his 1st child was born. I am really stunned that after all we said about teenage pregnancy that young people are having sex without protection. I can't tell you how many times I've discussed this with my children and grandchildren. As the saying goes, you can lead a horse to water but you can't make him drink. When my son and grandsons were younger approximately ten years old we would have discussions as we were sitting on the bed. These discussions usually took place on a Sunday. When another one of my grandson's was visiting I have to laugh right now just thinking about a conversation we had. I said to my grandson do you know what statutory rape is, he look at me sincerely and said is that when you rape a statue? We all laughed because indeed we had discussions though we were talking about serious subjects we made them fun to discuss. I remember saying to my son what would you do if you were on a bus and someone was on fire? (This had occurred on a bus recently back then) my son said, stop drop and roll. This was the right response but yet no one on the bus told this young man to do that. I felt that seeing things in the media were worth discussing with the kids. If everyone in the school was talking about it, I wanted them to get the educational values of the issue. We even talked about what evidence item from the Monica case was used. They knew that it was the dress with semen on it. Kids are more up to date then we think so when we hear things ourselves we need to get their input on it. I said to another grandson what would you do if someone had a knife sticking in their side? He stated that he would pull the knife out and put pressure on the wound. I advised him that we should never remove a petruding object. This could indeed cause severe internal bleeding. You see today our youth are exposed too much to violence. So I said to the children if someone was shot and the perpetrator fled the scene what aid could you give the wounded victim. They all agreed to simply put pressure on the wound call for help and try to keep the person calm and warm. You see we can teach more then we think with simple discussions.

Speaking again about teenage pregnancy are they not concerned about sexually transmitted diseases? In my day we were terrified of Aids. Now Aids is down played but beware HIV is surly on the rise in the young community. The new crave of today is polygamy. We have sex with one person that have sex with three other people those three other people have sex with three more people so now we have how many partners sharing their germs? We all have germs ladies young girls, teenagers how do you feel about yourselves? Does it not bother you to share your partner, are you jealous? What will you do to compete for his attention? This subject unfolds many complicated issues. There is so much exposure via phones, via cell phones with cameras, YouTube and websites. Anything you can imagine is out there. Do we just get plain and go back to basics? Abstinence?

Going back to my grandsons, you see they needed loving comfort not sex. As I go through life I miss the companionship of a male friend. Sharing with a spouse a friend or significant other can be a stabilizing factor in our lives. Being there for one another is so unique. Picking me up when I'm down. Rubbing my back when I'm tense showing their love when I'm feeling unloved. Make my day, breakfast in bed, and a kind word. Things that can be so small but go so far. It's a proven fact that touch is needed throughout our life a loving touch.

Man is not an island. So what do you do when you never come into contact with another person (you can have a Monique moment and hug yourself). This is a growing problem. I have true friends at work that have been there for me in my times of need. Including the times I needed a non-committal hug. Hey, I'm for real. I would simply say to them I need a hug (smile). -But like everything else this is a touchy area. Some people want to give you more. I am a survivor of rape. So to approach me and touch me can be taken differently. One day a doctor came up behind me and hugged me. At first I almost panicked, defiantly I was startled then as I turned I realized who he was. I was still a little tense not used to this being done to me in the work area. Sometimes people rub your arm, hand, etc. some of us read more into this. Sometimes we are right. I can remember as teenager boys would be fresh and rub the palm of your hand. This was channeled as a sexual gesture. SO although touch is essential we must be careful how we use this technique. There are many displaced feelings concerning unthereputic touch, unwanted touch. Some people use this to be harmful, hurtful, and commanding.

I can remember when my son's father and I were at the end of our relationship. I can vividly remember coming home from work and as I walked through the door I could see hands coming at me. He would hug me and proceed to touch me. Gee! Let me get my coat off, can I breathe (I thought to myself) because of my sexual experiences foreplay is very important to my psyche. It wasn't his fault just my reactions. When we end a relationship sex can be a very trying experience. I personally must feel loved and wanted in order to have sex now and back then also.

My faith has been my shield keeping the faith has not been an easy thing to do when so many non-believers are throwing stones at you. They hide in many places they have many faces. Some have much prosperity. We find them in the church and other sacred sanctuaries. People used to say I sold my heart to the junk man. Now its she sold her heart to the devil. Trust me I'm not going there because this is not a subject that I am well read in.

Lord in the year of 2005 we lost family members close to us. We lost Blake, Bessie and Alvin. My brother never fulfilled his dreams. I don't believe he loved himself enough. Blake struggled to live he was a good jokester. He would make you laugh but he reminds me of a clown that Smokey Robinson was singing about, the tears of a clown. It also brings another song to my mind the tracks of my tears, baby take a good look at my face my smile looks out of place, and if you look closer it's easy to trace the tracks of my tears. I love that song because I can relate to that myself. A smile may not always portray your true feelings. Blake was always talking about how his childhood affected him. I believe Blake knew that my stepfather was raping me. I say this because my Stepfather was always harassing Blake or beating Blake for whatever reason. I believe this was one of the reasons he had disagreements with my mother and because he never talk this out I believe he had repressed hatred that ate him up. As Blake would always ask me for $5 I would always give him my speech get a job Blake or try to get on Social security and usually I would hand over more than $5. Blake I love you more than I ever said. I just wanted more of you than you were able to give.

Today is 02-11-11 for some reason I think back to 09-11-01. I was returning home after dropping my son off to school. I was at Forest Avenue at the top of the hill near Silver Lake in Staten Island. My car stopped at a traffic light there were two lanes going down the hill. As I waited for the light I could see across the water smoke billowing out of a building. The driver in the next car looked at me and I looked at him. As we watched the smoke we knew it was the twin towers. To my amazement the second building burst into flames. All I could see was a cloud of smoke. At the angle we were at we could not realize that a plane had crashed into the second building. I was in shock. I drove straight down to the Staten Island ferry area. I parked my car and retrieved a pair of binoculars that I had in my trunk. Now I can see directly across where the buildings were burning. Through my binoculars I could see little figures wiggling as they sailed through the air. It took me a few minutes to realize these were actually people. Well that was enough for me, I went straight home which was nearby. As I watched the television the First tower disintegrated before my eyes. I could barley recover from this event. When Oh My God! The 2nd tower disappeared from the TV screen. A sense of emptiness fell over me. For indeed I knew that thousands had lost their lives right before my eyes. I was stunned sitting in front of the TV Numb From then on my life had a new meaning for me. One day I was in the supermarket and 2 customers were arguing I could not hold myself back. I said to them there are more important things going on in the world. So I said to my son one day I will leave home or you'll leave home and I will not see you again. When I die do not get caught up in the body image, my spirit will follow you always. That twinkle of the stars could be me. That flicker of the lights could be me. Just remember you were left here on earth to proceed and progress in a world made by God. I do believe that I have done enough good deeds from my heart; but if by some chance I don't enter God's kingdom I laugh and tell my son, I'll be down in hell with the fire proof suite or continuous ice water that will enable me to do good, wherever my travels as a lost soul will lead me. Maybe I can help somebody down there find the right cause and follow the right path. You never know. In order to carry out what I believe God wants me to do I must care about myself more in order to care for others. First we must love ourselves look into our own hearts and forgive ourselves for whatever reason. Confession is a good thing for the soul.

Lord please forgive me for the wrongs that I have done the ones I realize and the ones I don't realize. Though this material is being rewritten today I think about how I heard on the news that you can make a confession on your IPhone. In the church it may be between you and the Pastor and God, but on the phone it may be between you, Face book and the hackers (smiles). People don't like it when you tell it like it is, they know that most people are willing to go nine yards who act like this. I am not a saint not a martyr just a person attempting to live in a fast growing world. I'm not a very religious person when it comes to going to church but I do go to the Lord mentally and spiritually. I feel a light shining down on me now. I will march to the depth of my journey singing, talking shouting his word, my word. Behold Lord I come to thee with my open arms, allowing your influence alone to guide me. Steer me clear of the negativity, attempting to surround the world. Please continue to send out your positive spirit landing on and within the hearts of man. Don't feel alone man for God is always upon you. Merely open your hearts as you unlock a door close due to sheer ignorance for there are men among us who have and will betray us and God. Seek the Lord command do not allow man to command you. What you feel is bad is most times bad. Just ask God to brighten your path and your footsteps will be forever lite. As I think back In history about men like John F Kennedy who truly fought for the under privileged, the eternal light that shines on his grave reminds me of the eternal light I seek. Abraham Lincoln who had slaves did fight for some rights of the under privileged. We must all know that when we speak out about certain subjects we make ourselves targets. God knows we need leaders not mortals. Once the evil elements realize that they cannot rub out, nor stomp out everyone, we have a chance to be heard. God I ask for your protection, because to be a speaker these days puts so much in jeopardy. We must be willing to fight until the end, fight a good fight for the right causes and the right results will help everyone. Man has been the judge of too much. Some selfish men lead other selfish men women, children in to lives that destroy what our country was built on. Though freedom for all was written many years ago. It has not yet been accomplished. We in our times have a chance to correct inhuman behavior. Man can be rich, first be rich in heart and your soul will be rich. I will dedicate this book to all those people who have influenced my life. From the backstabbers who taught me to endure to the positive thinkers who shared emotional perseverance with me. A man is not an island I have pledged my life and soul to the well being of people mentally challenged, physically altered and emotionally deprived. I have much focus to bring to the light one step at a time, with God's help I believe I can do this. I'm not telling you a story, I'd like to tell the story I'm living. Just take one look and see things for what they really are. A deep hurt can bare so much pain, pain in my heart; pain in your heart can kill. Pain turned in can cause stress leading to High blood pressure, Heart disease, Diabetes, etc… People know that stress is a big culprit in physical health. Chemicals are released in the body in response to pain and nervousness. Why do you think that a dog can sense when you are scared, there are chemicals released in our sweat. They smell it and start to bark. But when (as I have done we say get out of here and they are confused and don't know what we are thinking). Ever wonder why mentally ill people depressed people sometimes cannot look you in the eye. Too much is exposed in our eyes. Some of us have good poker faces, hard and cold. But most of us don't have it. Some people try to intimidate us by looking into our faces by looking at us in the faces with they're evil eyes. Some weak character people will back down. Because they are not used to standing up to this type of intimidation. How do you think a congress person can stand up before you looking in your face lying, it takes practice. Some of them even believe their own lies. These can be dangerous people who can lie and have a straight face. They pass lie detector tests because some show little emotion. How can a person do this? easy. Through life some children practice hiding their feelings to their family. This can be done so that they don't be continuously hurt. I was tormented as a child you'll never be anything, you're not like so and so, and why can't you be like that person. I would think to myself I'm me and I'm not so and so, let me be ME. You cannot let your guard down for one minute in this world. The negative vibes will overcome you. We must do our part to stamp out the negativity. To seek God's blessings you only have to open the door and ask him to come in. He will not be intrusive seek and you will find. Open your heart and he will enter. How come I keep being obsessed with God in my life? I'm trying to keep on a positive path. In today's world so many people are killing each other, children killing parents, husbands killing wives and parents killing children. With such turmoil it's hard to keep hope. Don't lose hope. We must keep our faith and this will protect. We need to love our children unconditionally let them know regardless of what they do they can speak to us. Boys especially have grown up sheltering they're feelings sometimes suppressing them. Mental health to me and others is like a cup of tea. If your cup is full it will spill over. Your emotions will spill over. At this time when your emotions over flow the closest person may be a target. Road rage reminds me of this. Most of the time they aren't really mad at you but because of stress you may have broken the last straw when you blow your horn, pull in front of them. You may trigger an over flow of emotions that you are not the initial reason for but you may become the final solution. So now they take all of their emotions out on you in retaliation. This is why it's important for children to speak about what hurts them freely. But everyone is not equipped to respond to children right. A parent is not a parent because they mothered or fathered a child we need to take parenting courses. Too bad this isn't done before you have the child. A lot of parents are from the old school thinking a child should be seen not heard. I can remember as a child my feelings were hurt, I began to cry in private to relieve myself. Some children become bitter and never cry just hold it all in the pain, the fear, etc.at other times in life their cup will over flow. We suppress feelings deep into our subconscious; that for some cannot be retrieved unless under hypnosis with a professional therapist. That field I became interested in because of my rape that I suppressed for many years. To forget the hurt will also black out some of our past. Our minds may block out too much. It's hard to block out selective information and retrieve others. Crying in silence I became very sensitive and understanding of other people's pain. At times that has been my downfall, caring a little too much for others not enough for myself. There are people who prey on people like me, they are called users. They never felt loved in childhood, and find it easier to use others for their needs. We as family have not provided good mental health, for things we did not understand about family members. Some family members kept special secrets, secrets of child molesters, rapists, etc. These people didn't feel protected by their family because the family was too scared to expose them or too ignorant. Not thinking about the problem was supposed to take it away it only made it worse. Now the person got away with rape etc. and was able to get away with doing it again, without the proper therapy. Years ago you did not talk about such things that did not make it right. So no wonder family members who were victims of assault, rape, molestation etc. kept it secret and as victims went also untreated.

I felt that working in psychiatry gave me on the job therapy. I had a curiosity as to why men raped as I found the answer out as I began to heal. I am not denying that I needed professional help. As I've seen too many not doing their job, treating a person with medication is not enough. No wonder the door is always revolving in and out. Therapist sometimes becomes empowered when they feel they make a patient depend on them. Patients need to be able to think for themselves so that when the therapist leaves or can no longer see, the patient, someone else can carry on. Mental illness has become less stereo typed even though it is not as publicized as it should be. We must embrace mental health and promote good mental health and do not scrutinize good mental health. We need medication for the mind as well as for the body. Let's embrace our responsibilities to the mind. Mental telepathy I feel will become more popular in the future. A capability in the future that one day we may all have if we live long enough. Vibes can be felt by sensitive people. I sometimes feel vibes that let me know how another person's body is responding. These abilities are yet to be explained. Hands on healing have been going on since the time of Jesus. Who wants to believe this when we have so many crooks? We watch some of them on TV every day begging for our money to make them rich. Poor people grasping at straws. Believing that you will get better is half the battle.

A murderer, a rapist must have accepted what he has done. He may never fully realize why he did what he did. Killing without cause is sad. Not that having a reason makes it better we spend so much money housing the criminals of today let's help people stay out of jail. I call out to prison personnel make a difference. I shout out to police officers. Some of you need to stop harassing people. Some of you need to be disciplined. You can't hide behind the law. This needs to be addressed properly. I see so much prejudice in the police department, correctional department and the health field. With our Iphone and Ipads, etc. we can take a picture of anything. Maybe we can stop some of the abuse if we click few more pictures.

Sanora Boyd miracle number one. Sanora is my second daughter and she always was different because she had her own style. Like her sister Tycia, she was an A student. They had the same father. I remember one night when Sanora was in high school, she didn't come home the usual time. So we went looking for her. Myself, Letitia and Tycia. After failing to find her we returned home. A car passed us throwing a knife out of the window, which struck Tycia in the ankle. Thank God the back of the knife hit her instead of the blade. This set the tone for my emotional state. Later Sanora pranced in the house like nothing was wrong. As I said previously, I wasn't a person who would beat my children. But my first response was to grab her by the neck and pull her down on the bed. Putting fear into her I stated don't do that again. I don't believe I ever had to do anything like that again with her. Sanora became pregnant at the age of 16 years old. I provided a roof over my children's head and financial stability. I worked two jobs but what I didn't provide was supervision. I tried to persuade her to have an abortion but I didn't hound her. Once she made the decision to keep the baby I let it go. She decided to move to Albany with the baby's father. She became an emancipated minor. I got over it and helped her as much as I could. She had the baby and continued going to school and was in a program where the baby could go to school with her. In November 1988 she was to meet me in Maryland and spend Thanksgiving with Tycia and myself. I had moved to Maryland with a boyfriend and Tycia was 15 yrs old. When Sanora didn't come to Maryland I simply thought that she had changed her mind about coming. I didn't know that she had been hit by a car in Schenectady, NY. Sanora was wearing black and didn't have any ID on her. She was crossing a street that led up to a highway. She was hit by a young girl who I am sure suffered a lot of emotional trauma. I was told Sanora landed on the hood of the car. As the young lady pressed her brakes, Sanora landed on the pavement striking her head. She was banged up pretty bad and suffered a subdural hematoma and was in a coma. In other words she had a severe blow to her head causing a blood clot which caused pressure on her brain. She was unidentified in the hospital as Jane Doe. It was on the news and the radio up state. The hospital put out a statement that if anyone could identify the young girl by the logo on her shirt to please come to the hospital. The picture that was sent out showed a swollen distorted figure. I cannot remember what the logo was but someone did recognize the logo. Well now I was in Baltimore, MD when I got the news that Sanora was in critical condition. I was a registered nurse working for any agency so it was easy for me to take off to Albany. AS I settled in on the plane. I can remember praying to god just let me get there and I know she will be all right (at least that's what I thought). I have told my children in the past that If I say I know something trust me, don't ask me how I know, I would just say I know. Thinking back a great grandmother of mine was said to be strange and psychic. Anyway, I arrived in Albany, NY and went to the hospital my other two daughters were with me. We were all at her bed side. Someone from the TV station interviewed us. Letitia, Tycia and Sanora were always rivals but don't touch any one of them for they all stood together. One of the interviewers asked Letitia on Thanksgiving Day if you had one wish what you would wish for. To my surprise she said that everyone watching this on TV would they pray for my sister. Tears came to my eyes. Sanora stayed in a coma a day while I was there. Then the shock left me and I became not only a mother but regained my nursing abilities. As I thought about it, I asked the doctor you have her restrained because she is on the respirator and it is helping her to breathe so you don't have to worry about her pulling the tube out but you also have her sedated how much coma and how much is sedation. I asked if she could stop the medication. He lowered the dosage and eventually stopped it that day. Sure enough she woke up the next day. While in the coma on the first day, I used to sing spirituals to her and hold her hand. She would squeeze my hand. When her breathing got faster I would say to her Sanora you'll be alright you can't talk right now because a tube is in your throat but relax it will be okay. She would relax and breathe easier. When I told this to the doctors they looked at me with skepticism. I worked private duty while I was going to school for my RN. I was a licensed practical nurse. I took care of many comatose patients. I had experience talking to them and singing to them. I would let them know what I was doing before I would do it. Some of the workers would look at me as if I was strange speaking to an unconscious person. Back then some people didn't realize that some unconscious people could hear. Though it had been proven many times after regaining consciousness Sanora would recycle numbers. At least that's what I called it. She would say 546474 go on and on. Sanora got better I needed to leave to go back to work. I would return frequently. I had sent to Staten Island for my brother Blake to come and live in Sanora's apartment visiting her daily. Later I found out that Blake slept in her room on the floor next to her each night. He was the best therapist she could have. He would encourage her to put her leg on the machine that would exercise her leg because she also had a leg injury. I had spoken to the doctor while she was in a coma. I had asked about the condition of her leg. He said to me her leg is stable but it's the least of her problems she would probably never come out of the coma. I said to him with the utmost confidence my daughter is going to come out of the coma. I asked to speak to him outside of the room for a minute. When we got outside the room I said to him, if you don't believe that my daughter will come out of the coma then I need to get another doctor who has not given up hope on her. I want a doctor to believe that she will get better, one with hope. He had said that maybe she could be transferred to a hospital in Connecticut. I thought to myself and where would I be.

That year a New York City jogger had been in a coma and that is where she was taken. I told him that I was going to be moving back to Staten Island, NY. I was going to be caring for

Sanora. Several incidents come to mind as I think back to when Sanora was in the hospital. At one point she had a low temperature so she was put on what is called a water bed. The bed could warm her plus prevent bed sores. The bed felt cold to me I had experience working with this bed in the United States public health hospital. So I knew the temperature of the water had to be raised before putting a patient on the bed. As I explained this to the nurse she went ahead and put Sanotra on the bed. Never the less within a few minutes Sanora was shivering and had to be removed from the bed. Of course at times other nurses do not take our advice how about read your manual. We professionals must act like professionals. Listen to the other professionals with respect. Another incident happened after Sanora had surgery because Sanora scraped her backside on the road when she was injured, she had a wound there. I heard the nurses telling her one day you can wear the diaper. Sanora had worn diapers after coming out of the coma because she had not gained control over her bladder. Urinating in her diaper. I believe this is how her wound became infected. She was taken to surgery to clean the wound out. At this time, I was in Maryland and Sanora told me this information over the phone. I told her that I would fly to Albany the morning of the operation because I didn't want her to go into surgery with fear. Though we prayed over the phone I told her that I would be there. The doctors and the nurses were aware of why I was coming and when I was coming. That morning I left for Albany arriving prior to her set surgical time. To my surprise Sanora had already had the surgery done. There had been an opening in the schedule. This was not my priority at this time but I thought we arranged a time that I would be there that she would have surgery; I was going to be there to alleviate her fears so why would they do surgery earlier? She felt that she would not wake up after been given anesthesia. She knew that she have been in a coma previously. When I got to the unit she had just been returned from the recovery room. I was told that she was awake but when I tried to awaken her she failed to respond. I shook her; I pinched her and no response. Sanora is light skinned but she was as pale as a ghost. It didn't take a genius to know that something was wrong. I called the nurse to her bedside she tried to take her blood pressure once in each arm upon trying a third time I told her to call the doctor please. The doctor came right away to the floor and was able to see what the problems were. Sanora had an IV giving her fluids into her veins. But the IV was out. IV fluids help to enable you to wake up after surgery. By putting fluid into your veins the anesthesia can wear off. The doctor started another IV and within minutes Sanora was responding and her color had improved. Sanora was hit by a car on November 23, 1988 because I knew that Sanora could probably hear me and others in the room. I tried to provide a safe calm and caring environment for her. AS she laid in a coma I kept people out who was negative thinking talking about how bad she looked and will she come out of the coma. I wanted her to hear positive feedback. I would say Sanora you cannot speak to me but if you can hear me have patience. She would sometimes squeeze my hand. I said, with God on board there is no doubt that you will be alright. Trust in the Lord as I do, for he will see you through this. It is very hard to focus on positive things when so much is going on. But we must bring ourselves into a given situation and meditate. Block out put out and cancel all negative interference to achieve a given positive response.

Miracle number two Tycia Boyd. Tycia Boyd is my youngest daughter. She was going to a community college when she began to have symptoms of a neurological disturbance. She was limping at times requiring a cane. She had become forgetful; her vision was disturbed at times. One day she walked across the street and on her way back her vision became blurred requiring assistance to walk back to her fiancé' s car. There was a time when she even called her fiancé by the wrong name (you just don't do that). Her nursing teacher told her that her handwriting was changing and she had slurred speech at times. I can remember she passed out and was taken to the hospital for testing. It was a long process that she went through to receive the right diagnosis. I can remember the year I went to the million women march; I brought her a wooden cane. We were close and at that time I helped her as much financially as I could. She was on welfare and was put through a lot of unnecessary stress. I could remember back when I was pregnant and my husband had quit his job I just needed help paying the light bill. I felt that I had to jump over a barrel and through a hoop to get assistance. The reception that I got at the welfare office was traumatic to me. They were so cruel at the office and speaking down to me. I was probably making more than the people interviewing me because at that time I was a registered nurse. TYcia had a good relationship with her future husband; although she did not know what was wrong with her he told her that he would not leave her. Such love and dedication. I prayed each and every day that her diagnosis would be revealed. I prayed that we would not find out on an autopsy. Though she took several test for multiple sclerosis; they failed to reveal her illness. She was tested for all types of infections she was even tested for a disease that is carried by cats. She was slowly losing weight I remember seeing her one day and thinking to myself she looks anorexic. I was stunned to see her size dwindling continuously. Then one day my mother was watching a TV show a topic came on concerning Fen Fen a drug used to lose weight. It was said that some of the users were suffering from heart disease. There was a number that my mother wrote down, Tycia called the number and sure enough a date was scheduled for testing. She had used Fen Fen briefly. This test was an echo cardiogram. When the results came back they were sent to her medical doctor. Tycia decided to come to my house and call the doctor from there. Since I was a nurse she wanted me to hear what was to be told to her. I was on the phone in the bedroom she was on the phone in the living room. I heard the doctor say to my daughter as a matter of fact you have a tumor in your heart the size of a golf ball. He told her to come immediately to the HIP center. Well you could have blown me over. Tears came into my eyes. Since approximately 1995 she had exhibited many symptoms. She was even told at one time she had a brain legion. At that time I decided to take her to the John Hopkins hospital in Baltimore, MD. We had been to see a surgeon on Staten Island, and he wanted to do a biopsy of the legion. The legion was located in the hypo thymus. This is an area deep in the brain. They had wanted to do a needle biopsy. My feelings were if this legion was cancerous any needle prick could cause the cancer cells to leak into the surrounding tissue. So this is why I decided she should have a second opinion. We went to Maryland that Saturday we didn't have an appointment just a lot of prayers and hope. I had asked everyone I knew to pray for my daughter. I didn't care what religion the person was. My oldest daughter Letitia drove a white jeep at the time. Before we left; TYcia's doctor had given me some medication for her. The name of the medication was Decadron. These pills would help in case the brain swelling increased. He told me to watch for sleep apnea, that if I saw her yawning constantly this could be a sign. After arriving in Maryland we drove up to the front door of the hospital. I went in and asked if I could leave a note for the brain surgeon Dr. Carter. Dr. Carter was a world renowned brain surgeon. He was black. Miracles have been reported to have happened in his operating rooms. A few years later he had operated on twins who were joined at the brain, they both survived. Someone I knew had given me his book to read. She was aware of Tycia's condition. This was truly the doctor that I wanted my daughter to see. I left a note and the next day I had received a phone call at our hotel telling me to call Dr. Carter. Dr. Carter told me that he didn't work with adults but his colleague was willing to make an appointment with me later that day. Well needless to say, I was pleased with this doctor, all six feet of him. He was a tall handsome white man; very nice and professional. He reviewed the x-rays that I had brought with me and suggested to me that the doctor do the biopsy. He reassured me in his way that everything would be okay. In the John Hopkins hospital lobby there was a statue of Jesus. We prayed in front of the statue before we left.

In the past I had worked at the John Hopkins hospital. I was very impressed with their techniques. When it came to diagnosing a patient with a mental disorder they would first rule out any medical problems that could have caused any of the effects. On September 15, 2006 4:30am I noticed that Tycia was yawning a lot. I prayed that her breathing would be okay. So we started our trip back to New York. After getting back to NY we went to Staten Island Hospital because this was the day that Tycia was scheduled for her biopsy. After arriving on the floor a halo was placed around her head. A halo is a piece of iron placed around the head. She had been premedicated with morphine. This procedure was still painful. I prayed for pain relief and that the results would be positive. Tycia cried in severe pain and as I comforted her I had to turn my head away so that she couldn't see the tears in my eyes. We went down to the x-ray department and x-rays were done to be sure the placement of the halo was right and to locate the brain legion. A few minutes later the surgeon came out to me and said, Mrs. Boyd I don't know what happened. We can't locate the lesion it has shrunken. Well I didn't know how to respond to the statement. He asked me, if I had given her the Decadron. I replied no it was as I spelled G-O-D. He said to me with a question in his eyes, what do you mean? Then I said to him it was GOD. I prayed and everyone I knew prayed for Tycia. I felt that the prayers of so many people were answered. This was one step in her getting better. I asked Tycia, Do you believe in GOD? She said, yes. I said if you truly believe in GOD then you must give this problem to GOD and don't worry anymore about it just pray. I have always told my children that true believers didn't worry themselves to death. Just pray and God would take care of everything. I realized that this was a tall order. But she understood what I was talking about. I also realized that there are times when people pray and prayers are left unanswered. I have not experienced this yet but like I always say I will never bury the living. As long as the person has a breath in them I believe there is hope. Tycia joined the church soon after that and she was baptized. As we prepared to go to the

HIP center I took her by one of my favorite stores K-Mart. I brought her a diamond cross. I wanted the cross to be visible on her. I wanted it to remind her of the faith she needed. Just like praying in front of the statue of Jesus in Maryland. The stature did not represent an idol it represented a feeling of faith hope and peace. She was scheduled for more testing at St. Luke's Roosevelt hospital in Manhattan. After meeting the doctor she was scheduled for the next day. Her surgery was of the most importance. Fabien became engaged to her while she was in the hospital recovering. He had asked for my permission. I felt that this would speed her recovery. I was reminded by Fabien recently that the day Tycia was diagnosed with Myxoma; he was in Manhattan paying off her engagement ring. He told me that I said to him are you sitting. Just listen to me for a minute. After explaining her diagnosis to him I heard Fabien say, "Oh my God". When he said that I yelled at him to calm down because Tycia needs you to be strong. This does sound like something I would say. Though Tycia had medical problems she had perseverance. At one point she was upset because she thought I would be disappointed when she failed a test. This meant she had to take the course over; she was at the completion of her nursing program. I explained to her that finishing school was not as important as her life. She pushed herself seeking A's I explained to her that she finished A or B she would still get the same degree.

She later became a substitute teacher because the pressures of a nursing career after open heart surgery were too great. All three daughters have shown great motivation. Tycia finished college in four years withstanding her medical problems. Sanora to get her GED months after recovering from a traumatic brain injury and last Letitia to live through her heart stopping, a stroke and open heart surgery. The doctor at St. Luke's Hospital said that the tumor that Tycia had could have disintegrated at the time of the surgery this would have caused a massive heart attack. He said that it was like jelly, one of those jelly balls the kids used to play with on a string. It was like a pendulum that swung back and forth in her heart as it beat. Tycia had limited her activity because she would be short of breathe. This saved her life; we must listen to our bodies. Pieces of the tumor had broken off logging in her fingertips and toes. This was shown as little red dots in the tips of her fingers and toes. Had she seen a cardiologist she could've been diagnosed earlier, I was told. Tycia's symptoms subsided after the surgery. Approximately a year and a half later she gave birth to a beautiful baby girl, Ashley Gensesis.My interpretation of her nameTycia almost died to ashes now she had a new beginning (Genesis).

Moving on to another subject concerning hospital Staff. You see I love nursing but God knows we don't have enough help to care for all the patients. Some staff is forced to take short cuts that can lead to incompetency. We as medical technicians don't always see the psychological needs of our patients. My daughter needed reassurance prior to an operation. Is this important? Could her being scared and terrified alter the operation? Terror can speed your heart beat. The cause in the increase of a pulse may not be known by the doctor. When we are scared of a dog or a fire whatever our adrenaline is pumping. During an operation we want the anesthesia to work. I am merely saying take everything into consideration. The patient's well being is extremely important. You ever heard the statement scared to death or she died from a broken heart. I learn a long time ago while studying the mind that body and mind work together or against one another.

As a person looks back on their life I would suppose they could see back to their childhood, unfortunately I have memory lapses. I remember in spurts, as they say dribs and drabs. Being raped at a young age of 6 years old has left me fragmented. As my life unfolds I do believe this will be explained further, I'm coming out of the dark in to the light. The person who raped me was named Harold. He was an ex soldier. I was told that he was in the war and suffered from shell shock. As he would think back to periods of when he was in the war he would wake up shaking, sweating and screaming. My mother would comfort him as best she could. That night that he raped me I can still visualize in my mind as if it was yesterday. The room was dark with the glare of the TV lightning parts of the room. I don't know how and why this happened but I woke up that morning predawn with him raping me. I never said a word; I just pulled the covers over my head. I don't recall what happened first, all I know is that I went someplace else in my head to prevent me from screaming. This is when it all began, denial. I would hum to myself giving me comfort. Children protect themselves by creating a safe place to go in their heads. So you see I know what it's like to block out events that are painful. Think in your head that you are someplace; deny your body the feeling that is happening. Of course its happening but I denied these feelings not wanting to feel this new thing. When having sex if you allow yourself to enjoy it, it's hard to be a victim; I thought. I can remember becoming rigid holding my hand over my breast to protect them. Later in life when he continues to rape me from ages 12-16 I realized that the breasts can give off sexual feelings not of your own choosing. I truly don't know how long he used my body at six yrs old. I know that he would clean my body up. Seems that this type of behavior didn't stop for a while. How could I tell my mother who was like a stranger to me, immature at most leaving her child helpless? I can remember when I was about fourteen years old that Harold was holding a shotgun and threatening to kill my mother. Well I had had enough. I remember standing in front of her and telling him to kill us both. He put the gun down, I don't know why. He knew exactly what I meant though she didn't. He knew I was sick of him raping me constantly while she worked at nights. I was afraid to sleep at night. Went to school tired. My mother would cook dinner during the evening before going to work. It was my job to heat it up and feed everyone. I guess this is why I never learned how to cook. It was my job to go to the laundry bring the clothes home and fold them and iron what needed to be ironed. I hated ironing. I can remember going to my aunt's house numerous times, my mother was beaten but she'd always returned. They used to drink most holidays and the day would end in a fight. When I was 16 yrs old I attempted to have a boyfriend. Feeling less than equal to other girls I was having sex with him in his car. At this time my mother and stepfather were working the night shift. To have a boyfriend to me meant having a person show interest in me. He gave me the courage and the confidence to speak out. I told him what had been happening to me and made him promise not to tell anyone. Things were becoming unbearable and I needed to confide in someone. I stayed out late one night and was afraid to go home. That night my boyfriend drove me to Brooklyn. I was looking for my father who I hadn't seen in years. I had his address but he no longer lived there. So we drove back from Brooklyn and I went to my aunt's house. I was 16 yrs. I told several aunts what had happened to me. But we all agreed that it was best that I went back home and kept my secret. We knew that my stepfather had guns and felt that he would kill us all. From that day there was a change in my life. I was now able to stand up to him and tell him no with vengeance in my eyes and say no don't touch me. I don't know but I think that my uncle Melvin spoke to him. I had only two years before I would be 18 yrs.old back then you didn't speak out about sexual abuse. Many people did not truly understand that it could never be the child's fault. My step father had a violent history. Bringing my mother to her knees many times almost killing her many times. There was a new look in my eyes. I believe I could have hurt him at that time. I could still feel him on top of me. I could hardly breathe. His breath would stink of alcohol. I guess the alcohol gave him the courage to do what he did. Some people would call this liquid courage. Later in life if I didn't feel that a man loved me, I was unable to have sex. For years I never had an orgasm. I did not know what it was until years later after a failed marriage. A boyfriend of mine was smoking marijuana I got a contact. This enabled me to relax and for sure I had my first orgasm. My husband had always said that I didn't love him and that something was wrong, what did I know? If you never experienced it how could you miss it? He knew I was missing my climax, you don't know what it is like until you experience it. Through all of my emotional physical and sexual abuse I can be a loving partner if i feel that sex is not your only want of me.

Life goes on. I became 18 years old, graduated from high school, my first daughter Letitia was born a year later. I was an LPN. I was not in love with the man that fathered her. I went with him on a dare. We were totally opposites. But you know as I got to know him better I got to like him. I was pregnant and he went into the service. I believe that he was in Vietnam when she was born. I also knew that another young lady was having a baby by him so I decided to raise my daughter alone. I wasn't the type to share my man. I had two aunts that would babysit for me. Thank God for them. In one way or another they helped me to become who I am today. I was never understood, I was a person who didn't always go along with the crowd. I had my own beliefs and was a true leader not a follower, I was a real rebel. My life has been that of a person barely living just existing. I got married to Quincy because he fascinated me. He was handsome and clever he wore suits and ties to work every day but what I didnt know about him until later that he drank on weekends. He was a weekend alcoholic. Alcohol gave him the courage to say things that he could not say; before I met him my life was bizarre. Going out on the weekends sometimes weekdays just not being too stable though I worked, I felt disconnected. After having my first daughter Letitia, I had lived my first few months with a sister in law. Once I found out I was pregnant I chose not to stay with my mother. At that time she was too critical of me. I didn't need badgering I needed love and compassion. I had a job so I didn't need her financially. Three years later being married my life had a sudden turn, my husband became unstable. Lost his job and became Mr. Mom. He was very smart and would take many courses. Usually quitting them before completing them. His mother was also an alcoholic. There is a thin line between alcoholism and drinking too much. This drinking turned me off. For the next four years I planned on leaving him our two daughters- Sanora and Tycia are a year apart. We lived several blocks from my mother so now with three children and a student it was difficult for me to do all my necessary chores. This is when it was decided that Letitia would stay at my mother's house during the week and come home during the weekends. Now I regret this because it made her very insecure. She was darker than my other two daughters that are very light skinned. Some relatives would call them white children I can remember when Sanora was born for several months she had blue eyes. The nurse even brought her to the white lady in the bed next to me. My first note that something dreadful had happened in Letitia's life was when we lived at 321 Broadway. Sanora and Tycia and Letitia all sisters were reunited. She was about 16 yrs old. I do remember Sanora saying to her; tell her. So I said, tell her what? Well now the truth came out that Letitia had been abused by my step father. She had been living at my mother's house with Sanora and Tycia when I first decided to move to Maryland. I had been looking for an apartment large enough for all of us. I never wanted to let my children live with an outside man. How stupid of me. It had never entered my mind that my stepfather was a child molester, a pedophile and would touch my daughter. I was young and dumb I thought that I was the target not all children. When I found out this information I told my mother who didn't believe me. Here is how I decided to run to Maryland. After graduating from community college as a registered nurse. I had started to work at a hospital where I met a young lady from Maryland. It was ironic to find out later that she was my son's cousin. This was the second time that I had moved to Maryland. Once I had learned that my stepfather had raped my daughter if I stayed in New York I would kill him. Let me just step back a little further. Before in that the first time I moved to Maryland I had met a young man from Honduras he was tall and dark, there was just something about him that I liked. After the decision that we were going to date I went to his one room where he left me alone. He was to return in an hour or so. As I lay down on the pillow on his bed, I noticed something hard under the pillow. I lifted the pillow up and to my surprise there was a gun. It was a large gun I believe a Luger. I immediately became afraid. No longer sleepy. I was afraid to move. It was as if the gun had a mind of its own, that it could fire and kill me without anyone pulling the trigger. When he returned I let him know that I was afraid of guns and that I did not want to see it again. As our relationship developed we moved into a house. I split my time between my mother's house and the rooming house. I paid my mother and we shared the rent at the rooming house. Well my rule of thumb was to give a person one year if at the end of a year our relationship didn't improve I would break the relationship off because truly I wanted to settle down. When I decided that he was not making any progress and tried to end the relationship he threatened to kill me. Truly I believed him. I told my mother that in a few weeks I was leaving and that she was not to tell anyone where I was going. I would later send for my children. Letitia came along and this is when I realized what a poor mother I had been. I had provided all the financial support but not the loving care. She cried because she did not want to stay in Maryland, I didn't know how to comfort her. I realized that we never really had hugged or embraced that much. My own mother didn't hug me or embrace me as a child. I had a different relationship with Sanora and Tycia because they hugged me a lot. Letitia had spent a lot of time with my mother. You cannot turn the clock back so after I was unable to persuade Letitia to stay I sent her back to New York. I stayed their only one year. That year I worked at the John Hopkins Hospital in Maryland. I had a choice working with sexual offenders or anorexics. I had worked at a psychiatric institute on Staten Island. I always wanted to know why men raped children. I was given a definition of his condition a pedophile, a child molester. Over 75 percent of people who molest were molested. I did not realize that he was a predator. I learned that these men felt more secure with children. Whatever triggered this behavior sometimes is never known. The unit I worked on was to give a seminar on rape. Since I had spoken to my coworkers they asked if I wanted to speak. I decided to present myself as a victim of rape. They taught me to become a rape survivor drop the victim title. Well as I presented my story I cried, got chocked up but realized how important it was to speak about this traumatic event in my life. To speak out brought much needed relief for me. It brought back meaning into my life. The more I spoke out about it the more I was able to deal with the feelings still harboring in me. I could never be a virgin bride. I could never walk and hold my head up and feel equal to so many women. I was dirty; this is how I felt for so many years. My experience there at John Hopkins hospital was a very good one. When I think back I have to laugh. I had been so stressed out the past year that I had not gotten my period for over a year. Don't you know as I stepped off the bus in Maryland, my period started? So much stressed relieved. I remember my period was a bad time of the month for me. My stepfather used to rape me then knowing that I couldn't become pregnant. I had run away from a boyfriend. I thought that I would stay in Maryland but later I changed my mind. I missed my friends and family back in New York. My exboyfriend was asking everyone about my where abouts. I was told that he had become very depressed being the dummy that I am I wrote him. He wrote me a letter saying that he was going back to Honduras and needed money. I agreed to pay his way. He came to Maryland to say goodbye. He stayed a couple of days and later after he left my daughters told me that he had asked them to suck his private parts; where does this end. He had threatened me a few times and I let him know that he didn't want to go to jail in Maryland. After he left I got the strangest feeling that he put some type of spell on me. Returning to my room since I lived in a hotel. I noticed the key would not turn the lock, strange when the manager came his key opened the door. I don't know what I was doing, I just knew that I was compelled to sprinkle salt over the room. I asked my daughters to pray with me. If he had created a spell it was my intention to ask God for his help. What an ordeal I had learned early in life to go with my feelings. So feeling that salt would cleanse the room I gladly spread it over the floor. I guess sweeping up the negativity was what I was doing, so I thought. Before moving to 321 Broadway in Staten Island I had met an older man 14 years older than me. He had helped to lay the foundation for some apartments that were not too far from where we lived. I remember him because he helped me lay the foundation for my life. He taught me how to begin to love myself; I guess I was around 36 yrs old. Loving myself didn't really begin until I was 46 years old. He was an old fashioned southern man, polite the type to open the door for you. His name was Paul. He had good values that I needed to learn. I thank God for our relationship. I missed him dearly after we broke up that was the second time I moved to Maryland. I had met someone 14 years younger than me. I was truly immature for my age. I had lost years because of my abuse. Tycia was a teenager than and after moving to Maryland she got a job and went to school. Sanora had become an emancipated minor and moved to Upstate NY. I was in Maryland for three years at the end of that 3rd year Sanora had gotten hit by a car. I was ending my relationship because as smart as my partner was he had become addicted to crack. Crack was his new woman. He had been well educated and was very good with computers. I began to realize what many women realized at those times. That living with someone who used crack is very traumatic. He would spend the rent money smoke crack in the house when I wasn't home and eventually lost a good job at the airport. Here I am a nurse and he was addicted to crack. I knew I had to get out of that relationship or I might lose my job, and my sanity. Crack was rocking and wrecking a many of lives.

My brief explanations of my children's life is nowhere near the broader picture we went through a lot together they made me become mature when I felt that I couldn't go on. I thought of who would care for them. You see in some form suicide is a selfish act. I admit that there had been times in my life where I felt that I couldn't face another day. But I never planned to take my life. You leave behind people who trust you, need you and love you. However at the same time I truly understand how some people who have been tormented all of their life can't put it together to love themselves. Loving yourself is not a thing you can just think about and do. This is easier said than done. Some people have the qualities that make them so self-centered that they lack the caring of others. It's a balance that has to be brought about. Selfish parents can't teach us sharing thank God some of us have outside influences. As adults we can make a decision who we want to be but don't forget it's the baggage we bring to our relationships that makes them fail. We can love our partner he loves you but due to deep routed pain that sometimes we are consciously in touch with, we can be hurt. A therapist cannot always unlock the door to our pain. Releasing these feelings that over flow into our future. We learn to respond in certain ways, it's not always the proper response to stimuli. Loving others is hard when we don't love ourselves. Sharing is hard when we never learned to share. Receiving is hard when were not given the tools of life. Life is a journey that is better traveled with someone. The ups and downs give us insight but we must learn to travel these roads with your head up so that we can see the rugged road. Many a bowed head is a troubled or person that is not fully aware of their surroundings (muggings, people hit by a car, walking into something etc.) I remember my youngest daughter's teacher used to call her grumpy. Calling a child names sometimes puts a label on them. She did have sort of an attitude but outside people and even people close to a child may not know the focus of their mental attitudes. My husband used to take my two youngest daughters to their grandmother's house while I was working. He would at times leave then in her care. Most times I believed she resented this because when I would come to retrieve them she would be very sarcastic to me. She made statements like I don't know why he left these kids here. I would usually comment please tell him that before he leaves them and I would apologize. I always left her a care package (beer money). She was an alcoholic who suffered from kidney disease as a result from the drinking. She didn't drink everyday but when she did she would over do it. I discouraged my husband from leaving our children with her. She is the one who taught me about passive aggressive behavior. She would talk at me not to me. She would make comments hoping I would over hear them. Children can sense when their care givers are uncomfortable with caring for them. They can feel unwanted. After a hard day's work at night I didn't want to deal with this type of distraction. I would say to myself someone please punch me, kickme, shake me or wake me. Not when it's over because I don't know if I'll be alive when it's over. The devil was truly working overtime in my life. My mother-in-law seemed to be an angry person. Only God knew what she had been through. I do know that she raised her son alone. At times I could feel my blood pressure going up, veins in my neck dilated and throat feeling tight. Trying not to act out, I felt that I could rupture an aneurism. Grandparents are sometimes abused by children who think that a grandparent is a built in baby sitter.

This is February, 2007 I am chilling out and my body doesn't feel right I'm jittery and I feel teary eyed. When this happens I know that I am over stressed. I will cry at the drop of a hat. Only because I can't punch a few individuals to get relief. I know that things like this could cause enough stress for a person to have a heart attack. When we tense up blood shoots through our blood vessels, how about a stroke, clot to the head. I tend to curse when I'm overstressed; this is why some people are very dangerous who constantly curse. Their words may inflict wounds on people. The anger can't be relieved by words alone and is why they usually then go into physical abuse. Cursing usually reliefs my stress but I am not proud of it. Verbal abuse can be as lethal as physical abuse. There are people who will provoke you to hurt them. Of course you hurt yourself in the long run. Guilt is a harmful emotion destructive in some ways. Shame is a self-absorbed affliction of pain. Pain can be felt as harmful. But for those who get used to it becomes (how you say it) hurt so good. This is why I would never say do unto others as you want things done to you (some people like to be hurt) Feeling hurt is the only emotion some people have or get.

In this year of 2007 let's learn some basics. We must work on ourselves and our children. Stop allowing passive aggressive people to take their anger out on us. These people do mean things to get back at us. They lose track of why they got mad. We just become targets for their unleashed aggression. What is the difference between them and a killer? They are slowing killing us, affecting our emotions in such a way that we go home thinking about what they did to us. We can't say and I say we because it has happened to me. I've gone home wondering why this person or persons are striking out at me. In order to defend or protect ourselves we now get caught up in the mix. We spill out emotions and don't get resolutions. I like the slang don't let anyone rent space in your head. Surely they don't pay rent. Psychology must be a part of our everyday lives in order to move forward in the world of today. Why are you doing such and such? What effect will it have on other people? What effect will it have on the whole picture? Let's together teach human rights from a young age. The old have so many barriers and find it hard to change. Open your heart and mind. Learn we must stop lashing out to hurt and destroy a weak and confused mind. People can be mean as they lash out not trying to solve their issues. Treat people with respect even if they don't deserve it by your standards. Hate creates hate. Love can at least create doubt. We were all raised under different circumstances different time's different guardians. Some people you would believe raised themselves. They are truly clueless. They never were equipped to deal with the changing world and times. Some take our precious lives for granted. Each of us has lived our lives experiencing a wealth of emotions. To get through or to go through life is necessary. Life is like a training and learning camp. Some methods and techniques are outdated, harmful and shameful. As parents we should have control over our children's lives. Once they become of age we hope that the control is bestowed on them. Many lose or give control of their lives to others who don't have their best interest in the mind or heart. Some parents never let go.

My son's father stopped by today and prayed for us. He knows how much I have to do and some of what I'm going through. Through all of this I sometimes feel I have life but no life of my own. I have a song in my mind nobody knows nobody cares when the tears fall from my eyes, do you think anyone would come and ask me the reason why no because nobody cares about me. I must admit this doesn't really apply to me because there are a lot of people that care about me. It's always easy for someone to give advice. I am not a hater but sometimes things are easier said than done. Certain situations are too personal for outside people to give advice on. Martin Luther King had a dream. I have a dream that people will start to love and appreciate each other. I have a dream that I will be able to reach a lot of hearts that have been forgotten. I have a dream that families will truly know the meaning of the word. To be a friend that will be there. An anytime anything person, there when you need them. Mentor be a helper to our children, help to give understanding to things unexplained. One who will help us to look for God's help? I am a person that is here for you and I will be there for you. I can be helpful in helping you seek a solution. Love you; teach you, the true meaning of Love. Love doesn't deliberately hurt, we need to show love don't take love in vain. I feel with you and for you. Yes we can all help one another because we have a multitude of knowledge between us. We need to share it. Yes we can make a big difference. Start with love and end with love all in between can cause much fulfillment. If you give you will always receive. Don't constantly reach out for help. Give something in return. Nobody is promised tomorrow not even today. Tomorrow may never come. We need to hold our heads up and stand tall. Don't get into caring about yourself so much that you do not see others. Lean on me but don't leave me broke down because you may drain every inch of life out of me. Don't live off my spark don't dim my light and don't turn off my shine. Let's all light up the world. If you have problems seek help. Our feelings are so important to us let your feelings flow. Backed up feelings can cause illness within us. Physical tired is one thing emotionally tired is exhaustion. Health can come in many forms. Have a healthy mind, healthy body and a healthy soul. This is where I want to be and what I want to promote. Body mind and soul. My medical psychiatric and musical inspirations.

Lord Jesus I call on you today for guidance. Please enable new mothers and old mothers and parents to be good teachers. Teach our children to be able to take change. Nothing is written in stone, yet some of our hearts are turning like stone, the coldness is felt by many. We go to work with employees who bagger and intimidate one another. Those people who come to work and kill colleagues are not all insane. We know that we should not kill another person physically but why should people kill our spirit. You come to work happy and in good spirit but because one worker is not satisfied they create havoc which affects many. We need to be thankful that we have a job. Misery loves company. Some people are so weak that they will go along with others even though they know the other person is wrong. Some people allow their spouse to kick their butts and come to work trying to kick someone else's butt. If people realized how mean and hateful they are it could be a bunch of suicidal people around here. Start taking responsibility for your actions. Be kind it won't hurt you it may save you. Hatefulness is a burning disease; it will eventually eat you up. Learn to love yourself if you can't love others tolerate them. It is a constant battle to live this life but as we learn more and more why we were placed here it will be easier to survive here. Having a goal, having a purpose helps the body and mind to push forward not stay stagnated. There are some people in this world who still and always will believe black people are good for nothing. Black sisters and brothers we don't have to fight with harsh words or readerick. We need to speak out with knowledge. Do we have to go around taking pictures of the abuses we encounter? Do we have to have videos flashed across the news screen? We have such good surveillance equipment we need to use it to prove points. Points that some Americans will still deny. Some non-blacks will always hate us, just don't hurt us. Mentally, physically, spiritually, or financially. March 22, 2007 with the coming elections next year non-whites can make a big difference. We are so used to banning alone. Latinos and blacks we can make a difference. Our united vote can sway a vote. We need to learn about our candidates get involved in the voting process.

Patricia Boyd, Registered Nurse worked in a nursing home as a supervisor three years, worked in a coronary care unit for three years working in psychiatry for a total of 22 years. I also worked in physical rehabilitation for 14 yrs and worked at Calvary hospital for approximately four years part-time. Mother, friend singer and humanitarian. Working for 43 years as a nurse has given me a massive knowledge. Today is Letitia's birthday. I celebrate her rebirth. The old Letitia is in my heart and memory the love has never once changed. My very being has been challenged. I have become a different person. A few times I have lowered my resistance to the evil pull of the world. God gave me the strength to overcome this weakness and blessed my soul. I was in mourning for Letitia and can now see past and through this. As we come to a realization on a conscious level of past experiences we can begin to heal. This is a pertinent thing that needs to happen. Whether it will or not depends on external stimuli. It is very difficult to focus on one or two things. We must be multifocal to achieve goals in a world that's consumed by a strong negative force. I just hope the negative energy does not shift the earth axis. We must stand up for and to those who use hatred, misunderstanding and self-loath and to those who conflict pain on others. There are some people who prey on the words of others. We get so involved in the things we do in life that we sometimes disregard the hurt we inflict on others. Not always on purpose. We must with the help of mental health professionals such as therapists, social workers, psychiatrists, etc. Look into ourselves finding out whom and why we are and why we exist. I've always been interest in the people around me. I try to live my life promoting good mental health but due to circumstances I see changes in myself.

Right now it's in the news about the Chinese young man who killed 32 young people and himself. At first no one could figure out why he did such a thing. He was never harassed like the columbine teens, who he thought he was portraying. When someone's very soul feels betrayed, hurt, humiliated and tormented it does indeed inflict a cancer into the mind of the host. A cancer that will grow if not subdued. Sometimes our symptoms are so intertwined that we don't really see the cause of the actions we have. Why am I interested in this article? You see I felt such an overwhelming lack of not knowing what we could have done. Now I realize that it is indeed up to all of us, as a human race to help others, those that do not believe or see that they need help. Is the acting out of those who are internally hurt really crying out for help, like those who tell us I am going to kill myself? We need to realize that there is a need for help for those who are showing abnormal behavior. We say things that we regret and get caught up in not knowing how to apologize. To apologize. Means that we have to consciously accept that we did something that was wrong. Some adults, children never learn to apologize. We need to indeed work on mental illness so that we can master it like diabetes and heart disease, etc. there is so much that we don't know about the brain. We will be able to in our lifetime to open up the door with a key that I believe God has given us. We must retrieve the key I believe we will find it if we only look. I used to and still love the song look into my eyes and tell me you love, love, love, love, love, Me.

In some cases a lot of mentally ill people cannot look into another person's eyes. Some mentally ill or mentally intimidating people can look into your face and you will see coldness in their eyes. Is it true that the eyes show part of the soul? Some say that the young man that killed 32 other people had a certain look in his eyes, walked with his head down. Is this a person who had good self esteem? Does he wear sun glasses to cover the pain hidden in his eyes? Some of the pain can be seen in body expression. At first we painted the picture of a monster than a couple of days later it comes out that he was tormented I am not trying to make excuses. I am trying to understand why as a society we wrong. As we look around there are plenty of people who harbor anger, we all have someone in our family who does this.

There is a thin line between love and hate. It's a thin line between good mental health and borderline mental health. Some of us live on the edge. So what happens when we fall can we pick ourselves up? How many people will be there lending a hand to help you. How many people will be there to kick the chair that is helping you to get up? People do horrible things when they think that no one is looking. A son killed his mother over the weekend. Children are killing their parents more and more. Do we just say that the world is coming to an end? Well until it does we still have to live here. You see killing and suicide can be contagious. There are those on the edge that read these stories and quickly without thinking clearing think I'll kill myself. Well some people can kill others quicker than themselves. Then there are those who are so self-absorbed that because they don't want to live must take others with them. Some say where is God in these individuals well I will never accept those who blame God. Years ago they used to blame it on the bosanova. We must take responsibilities for the things we do. We must be able to make a mistake and move on but sometimes these are not mistakes they are listed in the category of hateful horrible acts. After working in a psychiatric institution, I realize that at times we were only placing a bandage over erosion. Not really getting to the core. So will we really ever get to the core when things are not always visible? Just as psychiatrists look into his patient's past, how was your relationship with your mother, father and siblings? Do patients always tell the truth? Do they withhold information; like my sister always held my head under the water or my brother would experiment on me, touching my genitals? My mother would hit me very hard when she was angry. My stepfather would come into my room at night molesting me, etc.these acts can be buried in a past that one wants to forget. Forgetting doesn't make it. These events will resurface in other ways. Some people are so troubled that the initial event might get lost in a world of confusion. Then because years ago we failed our children by saying that it didn't really happen, you must forget that don't tell anyone how do you do that? Hold on to feelings and pain connected to the abuse leaving abusers untreated and undiagnosed.

On October 01, 2010 I was looking at the Oprah Winfrey show and they were talking about women with 90 personalities, another 20. These multiple personalities were put into play to protect a delicate mind. So it's only natural that these minds are tormented. Parts of their life not visible to all personalities. I cannot begin to explain this phenomenon. Our brain is surely a master at work. It has to protect our body functions, heartbeat, respirations as well as sort out emotional and physical trauma. We are a complex body mind and soul machine. My next venture is to include in my studies, the soul. The spirit of a person; our spirit is often broken repairing it is till yet another area not explored enough.

Many years ago I promised myself after being sexually assaulted and finally revealing the pain and suffering I went through that I would never hold in my true feelings again wrong. I have been doing just that for the past four years. Having gone through several life threatening situations with my children the last of which that pushed me into silence. A silence rendered in order to survive, a silence performed to create a sense of well being one that shifted my feelings deep into a mind that could be quite creative and caring. A mind that I can sometimes say I might disown. We take each experience and process it in our mind. Storing it for future play backs. Well my rack is full play back time. Yesterday I lost a most valuable friend. One who said what she meant and meant what she said. I fell frozen in time burying my inner most thoughts into the subconscious retrieving what was bearable. Acting out in life in response to stumuli was so automatic that a year later I can't even claim. Today, January 08, 2009 I feel compelled to get out of the bed and record these feelings. I have arthritis in my knees and truly feel that releasing some of my feelings locked behind a forbidden door, will help to unhinge the past couple of years that I have spent barley walking pain in every step. I started my nursing duties as an LPN since I was a quick learner I was trained in the ICU and the CCU.back then I would take charge at night of a four bedded CCU Unit. Kind of funny that an LPN could be in charge at night but during the day you were treated like a glorified nurse's aide. Believe it or not this was my wish to work directly at the bed side of patients hands on as they call it using my sensitivity to life as an instrument of healing. I have always thought that I had what would later be called a therapeutic touch. I had no formal training in this but I felt sensations in my fingertips. When I touch certain patients. I even felt sensations when I was near their legs, for example holding my hands close but not touching them, I would feel a vibrating in my finger tips. Years ago we had to give back rubs as part of the am and pm care. At night when patients were uncomfortable we would give then back rubs rather than sleeping pills. Many were able to relax. Some merely needed that personal touch some needed someone to stop by for a second or two to give them needed attention. Back then a lot of us went into the nursing field for that personal contact. We wanted to care for the sick. Many of us needed to be needed an appreciated so we were also nurtured. All my life, I have searched for love. Many times in the wrong places and certainly in the wrong people. I was giving too much and receiving too little but as I tell my children even now don't give for what you will receive, give for the sake of doing for someone else. God will always reward you. When I wake up alive I feel rewarded. Many people lie down never waking up. Many people lie down waking up but not truly alive or living. We as a nation must stand up and be stronger, stronger as an individual making us stronger as a nation. We have worlds to conquer the mind in this year has become so advanced some of us realized it because many use mind power to lead others. Be a leader first a leader of your own thoughts be able to participate in your own fate. Do not give up your will to anyone. This is deep and not an easy thing to do but first of all know yourself, many people do not know themselves. Reach out and touch is a statement that holds many meanings. Lend a helping hand. We must demand our politicians move forward for mankind not one man. Lately, I have made so many statements about management in the hospital setting but my thoughts are the same as many other peons like me, we have become so torn and worn that we truly need outside help to solve our problems. We need fresh minds to clean up hospital situations. We elevate people into higher positions rather than fire them because we don't want to see any one lose their jobs or should I say certain ones. Make people do their jobs or replace them with people who are qualified. You see I have a serious problem it is called a good heart. I don't want to see anyone hurt but right now I hurt myself. What more can I do accept reveal the true facts concerning hospital work for the sake of myself and those workers that care. We have an obligation to our patients. We also have an obligation to ourselves. We find mental health problems in staff members. We need to learn to recognize and seek treatment for those who thrive on inflicting pain, hurt etc. on others. We meet them everyday passive aggressive types won't stand up to you face to face. But will throw a wrench in your day every chance they get. As we solve problems we have to realize that there might be three sides. The right side the wrong side and the interpreted side. Two people in a conflict can be right in their concepts a third side might make up the solution. But a joint effort is needed. We need to sit down at the round table. Discuss problems as a team. Come up with a team resolution. Every opinion is important as little as it may seem with discussions the little opinion can be added to a large resolution. There are some believers that feel that arthritis is emotionally linked. These last five years since my daughter Letitia had a stroke have been an emotional upheaval for me. I have turned into a loner for the first time in my life. Finding it hard to share my emotions. Being unable to walk properly has impacted my personality. I'm overweight and I waddle. I do it to shift the weight from leg to leg this makes me a sight to see.

Breaking this frame of mind I have to laugh now. I have to share an experience that I had around Easter time a couple of years ago. My sister, I and Letitia were leaving the house after making some Easter baskets. As we walked out the front door, Letitia and Vanessa still on the front porch, I approach my car to open the doors. Before I could put my key into the door my grandson's pit-bull dog ran from the backyard. He wasn't a friendly pit bull. He ran up to me barking. All I could see was teeth snapping at me as I held one of the Easter baskets in front of me to protect my body. Get out of here, I screamed several times. Well what seemed to be eternity ended. After hitting him with the basket he ran back to the back yard. Being naïve, I put my baskets in my trunk and to my surprise I heard my sister screaming. I spun around looking to the front of my car all I could see were my daughter's feet sticking out as she laid on the ground. The pit bull was over her snapping at her face which she covered with her coat. Well do I need to say, I saw red (A real Bull) I ran up to her feet nothing in my hands and yelled to the dog get away from her or Ill kill your ass. Though empty handed I took a karate stance. I was ready to battle empty handed or not. I guess the dog got my message. I might have been foaming at the mouth because he ran to the back yard again. Now I was really fired up. Excuse me animal lovers. I was now a wild animal protecting my young. I snatched Letitia up and threw her in my car. I told my sister to give me something off the porch which she gave me rake. I also told her to give me a brick that she saw on the porch because I felt that he was coming back. Ready, I now proceeded to the back yard entrance. Naturally he was on his way back. I looked at him eye to eye. Turned the rake around thinking to myself that I was going to shove it down his throat. He now became the hunted and he turned to run. I threw the brick at him so hard it broke in half as it hit the ground. I now got in my car and went to find my grandson to get this dog. This incident was very traumatic to all three of us. It took me months to get over it. That dog had been chained up and taught to fight. He had also been mistreated at times. To him I was an enemy.

I have used prayers all my life every day and then at other times when I was troubled. I remember another time in my life when I needed group prayer. I noticed a sharp pain from time to time in my chest that felt as if it was going toward my back. I made an appointment and saw my GYN doctor. A sonogram was done and a small tumor was revealed. My doctor recommended that a biopsy be done. Being the cautious person that I am I told the doctor that it could be removed then it could be biopsied. I have always felt that any evasive procedure on a tumor could cause leakage of its contents into the surrounding cells. Well while I awaited my surgery I can't emphasize more the magnitude of my stress. I really thought that I was handling it well. That is until three things happened. I had been verbalizing it with friends and associates and felt on top of the situation. One, I left work without my winter coat, once I was outside I was too embarrassed to go back inside and get it, I just drove home without a coat. Two I went to work on my day off, that is a No No, and three I went to work and as I stepped out of my car I felt a cold breeze across my legs as I looked down to my surprise I had my long john pants on, no uniform bottom. I had a cell phone so I called the supervisor who suggested I use a pair of scrubs located on another floor. Sometimes it appears that we are handing a situation well but it was revealed to me that I needed a little down time. So fortunately I was able to take a few vacation days until my surgery. I went to church and asked the congregation to pray for me. As the preacher put his hand on my chest I felt a surge of energy being generated in my chest area. In past time when it was time for Tycia to have a biopsy done I wasn't able to reach the Pastor. Being unable to achieve that I then realized an important fact. I thought to myself why did I believe that a pastor or preacher, etc. could convey my message to God any stronger or more sincere than me? Why did I believe that the clergy had special powers that could transform their prayers straight to God in Heaven? I proceeded to pray for myself and I spoke to God as I usually did. This was a big turning point in my religious transgressions. I felt empowered. I began to pray more and more. Don't get me wrong I prayed even when I was not faced with a problem. I prayed and thanked God for each sun rise I was able to see. I believe that the ministry is one of those professions that require honesty. It is a profession because some high roller ministers work at the seat 24/7 and collect many benefits financial etc. so you see this is why I choose to go to church less. I am not able to look at a person who I feel is a hypocrite and preaching to me each and every Sunday. I guess I have a one tracked mind. You do something that displaces my faith and I lose faith in you.

My grandson Isaiah has been a huge inspiration to me and for me. He has shown me unconditional love. Love I needed and prayed for. He has been the man in my life. He has built up my creativity and laid my sorrows to rest. Sometimes we get engulfed with our own so called troubles Many people will give you advice but few can reach you. Children have a way of uplifting your spirits if they can't reach you, you are in trouble. Children are so unique. Sometimes they are cautious when meeting strangers or relatives who have a questionable sense of untrusting mannerisms about them. Kids know sometimes they can sense evil or meanness.

Today I have my mind on Japan this is March 18, 2011. I am so saddened about the past weeks event. To know that the country is in so much danger has put a heavy feeling on my heart. My prayers are with all involved, the men and women who are sacrificing their own wellbeing to save their nation. I pray for all including an American soldiers and civilians stationed near and beyond those re endangered borders. This is not a Japan but a national, global warning. We must secure our nuclear plants to prevent future disruptions God help us all. At times we know not what we are doing or capable of causinig. Today is March 28, 2011 my goodness it was just broadcast over the news that rain water over Massachusetts revealed radiation. Each and every one of us needs to say our prayers daily. Get on your knees if you can (smile) I haven't been able to do this for years.

Calvary hospital, I must include in my writings when I worked at Calvary hospital, it is a small unit inside of Lutheran medical center. I stopped working there after Letitia had open heart surgery in 2005. I didn't have the strength to continue my work there. I enjoyed working with the patients though they were terminally ill. I looked forward to going there. Once letitia had her stroke I knew she needed me more. My philosophy is working with terminal ill patients was that whatever comfort I could give to them before their passing was a blessing. I felt needed there. I would sing to them, cry with their family members and give as much emotional support as I could to all including the staff. You see I felt well equipped with my psychiatric training. Sometimes family members were hurting as much as the patients. In my own way I would convey to them that time was of the essence. For my own experience I knew how important it was to let a family member know the love we have for them. These words need to be expressed while the patient is coherent and conscious. It is therapeutic to the family to express feelings to the patient as well as for the family member who is ill to put things in place before their journey beyond. I once had a patient who would light up when she saw me. I was always colorful. I wore scrubs and hair ornaments to match.

We often talked and I would sing a tune or two. She said that I looked like a breath of fresh air. One particular day I forgot to pack my hair ornaments up. I usually came from another job where I wore white so I would always have to redress. This day my patient said to me are you depressed? Without my colors on my hair I looked very plain. After that I never forgot my hair ornaments again. Her husband stayed with her all of the time unless he had to go home briefly. Then he would leave someone else in attendance. One day he said to me as she lay unconscious near death and in much pain. Do you think that I should leave and go home? He said that the other staff members had told him, that sometimes a person would let go if their family would leave. He didn't want to prolong her misery. As I looked into his eyes tears in my eyes I stated to him if you leave would you feel guilty if she expired while you were gone? He had told me when we first met that he would never leave her alone. Before he answered this question I said to him I know that she is in a coma but can I just sing a song to her? He gave me permission. The song I sang was what a friend we have in Jesus. He told me that that was her favorite song. I held her hand as I looked into her face, her eyes were closed and I could see a tear roll down her cheek as I song. By the time I completed the song she had expired. I could see a sense of relief in her expression. My voice conveyed the feelings I had for her. This event made me feel really good because her husband didn't have to leave her alone. Her suffering was now over. He would have no guilt for he had lived up to his word. He was there to the very end. This type of thing was what made my work fulfilling. I have always been able to deal with death in a responsible loving manner. I thank God for my experiences at Calvary Hospital as part of the team (I was an agency nurse). After working at Calvary I became aware of the hard work that goes into being a staff member there. You are faced with death each and every day. You have to keep up your faith in order to convey a peaceful atmosphere to your patients. Your personal issues have no place in a hospital setting. Our approach has to be truly patient oriented. This is why I feel those nurses, doctors, nurse's aides and other workers who come in contact with patients needs to be recognized on a higher level. We put firefighters, police and other public workers in another category. When they retire they can collect their pension job well done. What about hospital workers who also sacrifice their own well being dealing with the public when they're at their most vulnerable period. We need a better pay back plan. Why do we have to retire when we are half crippled, body and mind worn down? Where will the money come from let's explore that. My nursing career has been a forum for my growth. I guess that is why it is so hard to retired but now I am planning my departure.

It is now March 29, 20011, one fact I can't omit is that I was 41 yrs old and pregnant. I had felt that I would have no more children (wrong). I was gaining weight and my period was very irregular. I thought that I was in menopause. Well I found out shortly that I was pregnant. We were about to end a relationship mutually. I felt like it wasn't going anywhere. Once I was told by the doctor that I was having a baby I told my partner. I related to him that it wasn't necessary to stay with me. All I wanted of him was a father for my child who would be involved with him throughout his life. Well he agreed to help me care for our child. I knew he would financially. I wanted my child to have financial and emotional support. My son was supposed to be born in December. I went to South Carolina in Novemember to attend my grandfather's funeral. I had a deep emotional contact with my grandfather. When we were in each other's presence our minds intertwined. I had always felt for some strange reason that I was going to die young. Anyway after the Wake I went to my favorite cousin's house and my water broke as I attempt to get out of a lounge chair. My feet were elevated so when I bent over to push the chair back a pop was heard. I called Peggy so softly. Peggy then I said, my water broke. Peggy said, ok. After getting to the hospital and having the baby I heard the doctor say her pressure is low. I had a C-section since my contractions were causing stress to the embryo. What I did not know is that as they removed the baby the doctors had found tumors in my abdomen. They were removed Thank you again Doctors. This could have caused my premature death. So I really felt that even in death I was connected to by Daddy Reily. I had Paul on the day my grandfather was buried, November 11, 1990 on Veteran's Day.

Over 15 yrs before I conceived with Paul a fortune teller who was then a patient in a hospital I worked in told me after looking in my hand that I had 3 girls and was going to have a boy. Boy did I laugh. I stated I am not going to have any more children. She also saw something dark in my future, she appeared frighten. I told her don't tell me. Once pregnant with Paul, a patient kept saying to me I see a baby every time you approach me. Of course I said, Oh I'm not pregnant not even realizing that I was only weeks into that pregnancy. My path seemed to be casted a years ago Lord guide my future.

I must acknowledge all of my nursing colleagues and those people whom I came in contact with that simply listened to my many stories. Just listening enabled me to clear my head and face another day Thank you. Thank You to St. Peter's boy's high school personnel. Those I came in contact with or those I spoke to. You communicated a caring attitude to me. I want to shout out to the principle, I love you. You heard me so many times you made me feel secure and gave me hope that the boys were in good hands there. You and your staff including the coaches were supportive of us during our time of need. I cry now as I remember our moments shared. Family, friends, all my essential others. My love goes out to you. Please pray for me and my family as I pursue a change of direction and last but not least thank you to the firm of Amedura, Galente & Friscia, and the rest of the team that represented my daughter. Job well done. Thank you also Mr. La Rosa Lawyer and associates. These are my feelings shared with the public.

Patria Boyd, Dakoda Blue. World I have come please welcome me God Please stay with me. Here I come 1/22/12 thank you lord and all your angels and disciples. Please continue to surround me with your earthly and heavenly protection.

1 Can't buy me love (THAT'S WHAT THE BEATLES SANG). So many of us feel guilty concerning the outcome of our children. We blame ourselves for most of their misfortunes. We must let go and forgive ourselves. Moving on is a process needed in our lives in order to intercede the guilt bestowed upon our psyche. In order to rescue the young of today and tomorrow we must turn back the chain of events that have locked them into situations that render them needy and endowed. Some of them feel entitled simply because they came through our birth canal or by a C-section.

The slaves of yester years knew what hard work was. Though they received less than they put out they persevered. They worked hard for their money as Donna Summers said. Diana Ross said, "Reach out and touch some body's hand" not reach out and take from ones hand. Youth stop taking learn to give, a kind word, helping hand and a smile. If the emphasis was put on help thine self a lot of us could get further in life. We are in trying times if you have not learned to change your coping mechanisms it is time to start. We waste so much buying so many unnecessary things. You don't want to be seen yet you create an aura that expresses look at me. Another person cannot instill hope in you; hope is not a part of so many people. Become hopeful. Fill your mind with positive thoughts. It is so unhealthy to think about all of the negativity going on Get professional help we sometimes need it.

2We need to examine our own hearts and minds. We must not let depression take over. This a hard task to achieve. I for one have been plagued by depression on a day-to-day basis. Many of us are in the same boat. Let's stop the pretense. We are in severe trouble. Nature has turned its most lethal disasters loose. Is this not a coincidence? As we think about the world end predictions we must also consider if we can restore order. Just look around you and observe the tell tail signs of a deteriorating generation. Hate has created so much chaos in our once near stable environment. Pulling together, problem solving as a nation, as a universe is the only cure for an epidemic of anarchy. I really don't know why I used the word anarchy but maybe it will be revealed to me later. Go, our Lord and Savior please lend me your ear, instruct me and use me as a vehicle of knowledge. March 23, 2012 today's world of high technology has created pressures that we ensue daily. Minor problems now appear overwhelming. Once the economy got out of whack, people who thought they were home free financially are seeing a new day. They now join the struggling with many who live from pay to pay. They now barely meet the minimum requirements to sustain life. Life is now a challenge. The gap between the middle class and the poor is rapidly closing. There have always been entrepreneurs who have given to many needy charities. Now their home front is under attack. To think that the rich need to help is reaching far in most cases. Some do, some will and many won't. The wealthy are gaining a new stamina. Some of their noses are becoming pointier and reaching for the sky as they feel the power (smile). The only thing God has the last say. How many wealthy individuals are on the food stamp line? Recently a lady was in front of me in the grocery store who didn't know how to use her new found source of income. Her mannerisms and clothing leaked out of a sense of previously well off. Looked unsettled, bring attention to her.

3My great grandfather Henry was the product of a white father, who was the slave owner and a black mother who was one of his slaves. To think that the white back then and some now publicly despised blacks, they had the nerve to have sex with them behind closed doors. Today men still get off their heavy loads on women they share no feelings for. I wonder if my great-great grandmother's partner (if she had one) knew that the owner was bedding her. Oh well, water under the dam. We can never say we knew how these women felt. Preyed upon by an owner who thought of you as a possession? Women, are we not possessions today? As I think now in retrospect there is really no wonder some of our young men seem to never grow up or mature. How often some treat the young female like possessions, not even a prized possession. Some act as if women are put here to take care of them. This mentality must be changed in order to provide for a healthy offspring who will grow up loving women and not beating them down mentally and physically. Though we can understand the strain of being a black male in today's America it is no reason to down women. Women have been the back bone of the family for years, centuries. Being the bread winner is important but the aspects of life go far beyond earning a dollar. One cannot erase years of economic and emotional beat down. We must lift up our heads, mind and let the spirit flow into our hearts. Let's create a better world environment. Blaming problems on different things has not brought about change we must work this out and gain self-respect, self confidence, and self reliance. July29, 2011 as much as I feel that I have felt that I have moved forward I realized that I have stood still. I've traveled nowhere at all, simply going up and down the stairs. I felt that success was in my reach though I lacked the skills to advance. I'm please with the Lord who opened up my mind and soul healing my bodily wounds. I feel constantly at war. I yearn for a soothing calming effect on my being. I seek the resources and intelligence needed for my worldly acceptance. As we help others the lack of acknowledgement constantly pulls on our very existence causing so much turmoil. Lord lift my head up invade my spirit expose the negativity forcefully surrounding me. Deliver me from evil let your love light shine on me and place me in your ever loving arms.